# The Tiber Afire

Fabio Della Seta

# The Tiber Afire

Translated by Frances Frenaye

The Marlboro Press

Originally published in Italian as
L'INCENDERE DEL TEVERE
Copyright © 1969 Editore Celebes, Trapani.

The publication of the present volume is made possible
by a grant from the National Endowment for the Arts.

Manufactured in the United States of America

Library of Congress Catalog Card Number 90-60882

Cloth: ISBN 0-910395-63-2
Paper: ISBN 0-910395-72-1

THE MARLBORO PRESS

MARLBORO, VERMONT

To Marcella Tilles Della Seta

# CONTENTS

There are three things that are never satisfied, yea, four things say not, It is enough:

The grave; and the barren womb; the earth that is not filled with water; and the fire that saith not, It is enough.

Proverbs, 30 : 15-16

# PREFACE TO THE AMERICAN EDITION

*Habent sua fata libelli*—every book carries its fate within it. These words of an ancient Roman writer fit *The Tiber Afire* perfectly.

These pages were written many years ago, and many other years had already gone by since the events they recount. I was first urged to write them by a Catholic friend who was curious to learn what had befallen the Italian Jewish community during the Second World War. When all was said and done, the story turned out to be limited to a small part of that community. Moreover, it was addressed to a girl who had taken part in the student protests that erupted in the late 1960s all over the world, as well as in my city of Rome.

The preface to the original Italian edition of *The Tiber Afire* takes the form of a letter, which is not reproduced here because it is too closely connected to the people and events of those days of protest and the tumultuous confusion of ideas that then prevailed. The following passage now seems particularly obscure:

> I have come to think—speaking very personally—that in whetting our illusions and resentments, we neglected too long to look in the direction where we could have recognized the enemy at once and possibly faced up to him. I mean within ourselves. I feel, although I can't prove it, that when we understand how much of Fascism

(but this is only a figure of speech: better to call it the instinct to dominate) lingers on in each of us, we shall have taken a great step forward, probably the decisive step. Even though it seems to me quite obvious that you who come after us will have to face up to the same problem.

And yet it was this passage that caught the eye of at least one of my readers, one whose opinions I consider particularly important. And here was one of the first signs of what was to be the book's fate, that is, to attain its goal despite all skeptical pessimism and reasonable hope.

*The Tiber Afire*, a quasi-novel as I came to call it, was literally wrenched out of my hands by a young professor who, with little experience but great enthusiasm, had set up a small publishing house in Trapani on the west coast of Sicily. He had just issued *Rivedere Petra*, a collection of my short stories, which was selling well, and without giving me a chance to reconsider, he told me he would also publish *The Tiber Afire*.

The manuscript was sent to the printer; the pages were bound. As in the case of *Rivedere Petra*, the pupils of a painter friend made a number of sketches for the jacket and I chose the one I thought most appropriate. Many friends, in Rome as well as at the Sedeh Eliyahu kibbutz in Israel, were waiting for the book. But *The Tiber Afire*, just off the press, never reached the bookstores. Neither I nor my closest friend, who had been eagerly awaiting it, ever saw it in a bookstore window. The publisher in Trapani had overreached himself and had suspended his operations just in time—on the brink of the abyss, so to speak. I was much soured by the experience, and it took several years to be reconciled with the would-be publisher. Today he is once again a good friend, if a bit absentminded and subject to a few peculiarities (for instance, he refuses to take the plane to come and see me in Rome), and like many of us he is disillusioned with his former political enthusiasms, but responds more than ever to the appeal of literature and art.

My undue bitterness has faded with the years. Not simply because the passage of time has softened expectation and impatience, but chiefly—and here I come to what seems to me the extraordinary fate of *The Tiber Afire*—because, in spite of everything, the book has won broad recognition. How it traveled to faraway countries and fell into the hands of unexpected readers unknown to me, I have no idea.

This is how things went for about twenty years, after the book's first, fleeting appearance. Until one day, in a lecture hall in Boston, a remarkable American student of contemporary history, Susan Zuccotti, spoke at length on her research for her book *The Italians and the Holocaust: Persecution, Rescue, and Survival*, a thoughtful study of the Italian attitude toward the Jewish community.

It so happened—and don't ask me why—that *The Tiber Afire* and its author were mentioned several times in both the book and the lecture. And—still more surprisingly—it also happened that there in the hall, taking part in the discussion, was someone who appears in *The Tiber Afire*, now a mature and charming woman long resident in America, who had certainly not forgotten the details of the book and whose relationship to its author would at present be too hard to explain.

This then is how, and by what strange paths, *The Tiber Afire* has come to be published in the United States, thanks to the combined efforts of several people: that charming woman, an able literary agent, a practiced translator, and, of course, a courageous publisher.

I need only add that the present edition bears a new dedication, to Marcella Tilles Della Seta, the author's beloved sister-in-law, who died unexpectedly in Milan on July 28, 1988. May her memory cast a blessing on this book, for which she had great hopes, and on its characters, both living and dead.

FABIO DELLA SETA

Montevideo, June 18, 1989

# THE TIBER AFIRE

# I / VILLA CELIMONTANA

The stifling summer heat still hung in the autumn air, but the Villa Celimontana, a stone's throw from the Colosseum, promised a green and sober welcome. After the Via Labicana, a wide street led upward, affording a glimpse of the villa, half hidden by trees. The tram, from Tiburtino to San Giovanni, had passed through the most populous neighborhoods in Rome and skirted the Piazza Vittorio. It had stopped between two of the ancient hills, the Oppian and the Caelian, and there the adventure began.

As he approached the building, he tried to picture his new companions. He imagined them as stuck-up and disagreeable, to what extent he still didn't know. That's just it, he thought, I'll have to put up with the smartest and most conceited ones from all the schools in Rome. Everybody knows there's a smart kid in every class, and it's almost always a Jew. And what's a Jew? Someone who's excused from the class in religion. And why is he excused? Because his parents insist.

That summer, however, his idea of a Jew had begun to expand. It was during those months that he, a Jew, had become a hero, the protagonist of front-page stories in the newspapers. Within the family circle—relatives and friends whose existence he had not even suspected—the matter had not been well received. There were worried faces to be seen, alarmed remarks to be heard. "It's a moment of madness, it'll soon blow over." "No, no, this time they mean business."

A distant relative, who had fought in the First World War, could not bear the uncertainty and blew out his brains with his old army pistol. A huge throng of friends and acquaintances came to the funeral, as did the regimental band, which, in the opinion of grandmothers and aunts, played a splendid funeral march. That looked like a good sign. Other distant relatives, members of the Association of Former Royal Grenadiers, stepped up their guard duty at the tombs of the Italian kings in the Pantheon, a cherished old custom and now possibly a useful one besides. Mussolini, after so many declarations and strident victories, might have gone out of his mind, but surely the king would think differently.

Those who had decorations connected with the war or the rise of Fascism generally demonstrated more calm than others. Indeed, they sometimes flaunted an irritating superiority. "I have a silver medal, and I've been a party member since 1924—nobody's taking my cleaning woman away from me." People envied a certain major in the Quartermaster Corps who had served in Spain: lucky man, he'd looked international Bolshevism straight in the eye and now could brag about it.

But this business of the schools was hard to take. No Jewish child, whether his father had a gold medal or not, would be allowed to set foot in a public school. For the moment, this was what was most distressing. His grandparents, who lived in the provinces, sent a telegram: "Close to you with all our hearts." Something out of a tragedy, disproportionate to the occasion. Because to him, there was nothing tragic about it; quite the contrary; in many respects, the unfolding events were reason for pride.

Pride is a heavy word and may seem excessive. Yet it's the right one, exactly right, in every way. To be separated from the herd and rejoice in it, to aspire indeed to an even greater solitude—that, precisely, is pride. It was the same sort of pride that had driven the fourteen-year-old boy, in that splendid summer interval, to seek out the most secluded rocks at the seashore and immerse himself in the contemplation of seaweed and crustaceans; to envy the hermit vocation of *Pagurus bernhardus*, and the crayfish, which retreated slowly and sluggishly, except when for no reason they took sudden leaps backward or sometimes to the side; to enjoy the monotonous but infinite fluctuations of the tide, water against water, water against pebbles, against the rocks, against floating seaweed, always to the exclusion of any sound human in nature or origin; and to savor the sun, the light breeze, and the silence, without ever feeling the slightest wish to share them with any fellow creature. Even if the worst should come, he would keep it all for himself. This then is pride: confidence, the pleasure of always being able, with luck, to be self-sufficient, and the treasures of the mind, which no one can take away from you.

This was why, despite his parents' laments, he had found the new and unexpected trial acceptable. A singular mark of distinction, a unique opportunity, never to be repeated, to build one's character. The great exploits recorded by history had always been undertaken in a climate of adversity, the only way to leave timid, hesitant, mediocre souls behind. It even crossed his mind that such a golden opportunity was not fortuitous, and that the leader of the Italian nation might be attempting through a bold experiment to refine a splendid new amalgam, capable of withstanding much tougher battles. As though this were his real thought: let's take a Jew and make a man of him, indeed a peerless man, to be handed down to the future, the best and strongest of all, capable of surviving and of asserting his power over others. The just and invincible man, drawing strength and morality from nothing but his own inner conviction, as the political-science teacher says, political science being the science of governing men, and one that cannot be sufficiently praised.

But now the disconcerting and unwelcome conclusion was that he had clearly not been singled out for this privilege. The school, on the inside, looked like any ordinary school, with just a touch of picturesque disorder. Someone had hastened to hang portraits of the king and the Duce in all the classrooms. They may well have pondered the idea of adding a crucifix. Their concern had obviously been to create a school as identical as possible to all the others, while enjoying little confidence in the results. The teaching staff seemed to condense all the pedantry of the Italian educational system; their one aim was to announce to the pupils: "We'll pick up where we left off." As for his classmates, nothing about them suggested that they were destined to perform any outstanding, much less heroic, deeds: awkward fourteen-year-old boys in ugly shorts and brown jerseys, pale girls, their hair too long and blending with the black of their smocks. Boys and girls both seemed to want to be conspicuous, to be noticed, as though their sunken, watery eyes, constantly wandering in search of a place to alight, weren't enough to call attention to them.

Actually there were two elements that set this school apart from all others: the principal and Romeo the janitor.

The principal appointed by the Ministry of Education came from the Fascist Farnesina Academy, where he was said to have taught gymnastics. He was a swarthy young man with curly hair and a pair of very dark and darting, not to say shifty eyes. He could have been taken as a perfect example of a traditional Jewish stereotype, as well as the living personification of Fascist activism. It was known, however, that he was not a Jew, just as it was later learned that he wasn't a Fascist either. He was a quiet man, intent on doing the job with which he had been saddled, without causing any problems or having to endure any. But he inspired fear, and his presence was enough to galvanize the scattered forces that had come together in the school.

As for Romeo the janitor, he was an original, created through a long and conscious manifestation of will, since it is impossible, or so it seemed to everyone, for nature to produce anything like him by spontaneous germination. Fat and smiling, he had the ability to regale the students with his countless misfortunes, the problems of raising an unduly numerous family, and to make his listeners laugh at the telling. One always arrived early at the Jewish school and went home very late because of Romeo the janitor and his endless and highly prized stories, told in true and resounding Roman dialect. It was life itself that came from his lips, meaning the infinite expedients to which a poor devil must resort in order to survive: the sale to strangers of three bolts of cloth left at his house by a relative drafted into the army, as well as a number of supposedly woolen undershirts—made from some unknown material that stuck to the skin, they were therefore called *carabinieri*. Then there was the sale of chaplets and rosaries in front of Saint Peter's, in keeping with a tradition that would have Jews to be among the principal suppliers of sacred Christian objects. It wasn't clear whether Romeo himself had ever resorted to such expedients; in fact, it was doubtful, judging by his honest open face and the ribbon pinned to his uniform that spoke of military decorations. Nevertheless his stories were useful to those who were only beginning to suspect that life could be a difficult problem.

Romeo's masterpiece, his gala evening (which took place, however, early in the morning), was a *Kaddish* said in memory of Mussolini. The Duce was still very much alive, but Romeo the janitor, ignoring the prudent misgivings of his listeners, had already pronounced his death sentence and intoned over him the traditional Jewish prayer for the dead. This recital involved a kind of ceremony, with the students begging Romeo to perform and then promptly forming a circle around him, after having made sure that neither the principal nor any teachers were in sight. But even this circumspection added to their eager delight.

Once the audience was in place, Romeo put on the black cap that he always carried with him, and began chanting in the rhythms of the synagogue, unfamiliar to most of his listeners, the refrain: "*Yitgadal veitkaddash Sheme Rabba . . . ,*" meaning, though it escaped almost everyone, "Magnified and sanctified be His great name." The rest of the declamation likewise sounded strange to most, who were only prepared to grasp the turn of phrase containing the appeal "*ve-ne-fesh Benito Mussolini,*" that is to say calling down blessings on the soul of the dictator, whose imminent death Romeo foresaw or at least wished for. Indeed, in his eyes, it would have been a highly desirable thing had it already happened, for then all the fear and pain would have been dissipated for good.

Some felt it was not only a dangerous joke, but a silly and superficial one, a typical product of the ghetto mentality. But the fact remains that by arousing laughter Romeo achieved results that were not to be despised: he taught his listeners that the time had come to lay aside their illusions, while further warning them that one had to take a stand, fight, and if necessary hate. Furthermore, as a by-product no less valuable, a bond was established among the still divided and bewildered adolescents. A bond that in time would become something else.

A few signs of friendship were beginning to emerge. Not all the students had once been first in their class, either in conduct or scholastic performance. The prodigy of all time, the example lauded by all the teachers in Italy, had yet to arrive from Ancona. On closer inspection, there were even a few downright stupid and insignificant boys, who not by chance were the most likable and best dressed, able to sing the latest popular songs and versed in all the stock phrases for making advances to the girls. Among whom—except for the robot Giuliana, who did nothing but nod her head incessantly to whatever the teacher was saying—one began to notice some who weren't bad-looking. Generally speaking, it was good form to pretend to despise them, because of their idle chatter and their preoccupation with matters of no importance. But their company was by no means distasteful, if only to display the macho attitudes of some, among whom Vittorio was in the forefront. He, short in stature but of a more than usually well-developed build, and with blue eyes and blond hair, liked to insist—not without reason, one must admit—that a great part of the racial hatred directed against Jews was the result of their attachment to certain traditional modes, both physical and spiritual. He, a Jew by accident, as attested by his principles and his somatic features, was well aware of what it was incumbent on him to do: cultivate his own physical aptitudes, indeed increase them by the most strenuous exercise, in anticipation of the day when the whole nation would consent to make the comparison. In some supreme sporting event, or in the ranks of a fighting army: one or the other, it hardly mattered which.

It was he who got many of the other students to ride bicycles to school. For most of them, this meant crossing the whole city, but also being able to save the tram fare given them by their parents and spending it on their first cigarettes. Nor was that all. It didn't take long for bicycling to became a welcome exercise, which led to taking longer and longer routes, soon even outside the city. Since on Saturday and Sunday there was no school, the four or five boys most eager to imitate Vittorio embarked on ever longer bicycling excursions: fifty, then a hundred, and up to as much as two hundred kilometers. It was good exercise and served many purposes. It took one's mind off such troubles as one's parents and—no less irksome for adolescent boys—the thought of girls, and engaged the muscles till they ached. It also stimulated a huge appetite, and this facilitated the consumption of quantities of white, or preferably red wine, since everyone knows that to be able to drink and not show the consequences is the prerogative of grown-ups.

Another sport that came into vogue through Vittorio's efforts, though the participants were fewer, was boxing. Aside from the money to buy a pair of good boxing gloves, other gifts were required that not everyone possessed. Like landing heavier punches each day, and receiving them without flinching. And more often than happened to professionals in this noble art, you would be hit in some vital part of your anatomy. You staggered, put one knee on the ground, and waited for the shock to pass. But this, albeit tacitly, was allowed. It was eloquent proof that you were learning to suffer. Sometimes the blows caused real pain. But to these pugilists, suffering seemed like a real necessity, at least on the physical plane. This was a secret reserved for the very few. When the time came, there would be those with the spirit and physical stamina to resist.

These were the days when the newspapers carried, in bold headlines, the many regulations concerning the Jews—too many for the Italian temperament to be able to take in and apply. Aware of this deficient aptitude, the most skilled government propagandists were led to expatiate every day on the virtue and necessity of these laws. Hard to say what influence these incitements to hatred had on the minds of their readers. But in the young Jewish students, they aroused a great and well-justified fear, along with a desperate urge to resist.

No one knew how it started, but a rumor was going around

that the Fascists intended to take it out on the students of the Jewish school. Unable to pin down the source of the rumor, the staff recommended some elementary precautions: avoid eye contact; don't linger after school; go home quickly, singly if possible rather than in groups. All this helped to rekindle the rumor, and now even the date supposedly chosen by the Fascist interlopers was specified.

It was then that the little group of sports enthusiasts decided that the moment had come to display their prowess. Someone with more alacrity than the others got hold of some stout pieces of wood and fashioned them into billy clubs. With immense pride, the students practiced hiding them under their overcoats, and still more uncomfortably during classes, under their sweaters. No matter what the teacher may have been talking about, one's mind was on that hard presence, which was nevertheless a comfort: it dispelled the fear of attack and, even more effectively, the boredom of Latin syntax.

By the time the day signaled by this widespread rumor as the one destined for the slaughter arrived, every moment had gone to heighten the importance of the episode. The students were dismissed from school with renewed recommendations to keep calm. Everyone nodded, pale and serious, including those who had promised themselves to put up a fight.

It was a gloomy autumn day, of the kind seldom seen in Rome. The sun stubbornly refused to shine, the rain to fall. Unlike other days, the janitor Romeo accompanied the students a short distance beyond the gate, as though to say: I'll go with you as far as I can; I'd like to share your fate; you're not exactly my children, but in this awful moment I wish you were.

The group set off, as agreed, each individual a few paces from the others, but keeping an eye on who was ahead and who behind—this too had been agreed upon, without telling the teachers. They skirted walls with the unexpressed purpose of taking refuge inside a portal should the worst come to pass. This was not to avoid the fight, which would have been impossible anyway, but to hide from the stares of the inevitable onlookers who would come running.

All of a sudden, the students realized that by skirting the walls they risked coming within range of a bunch of young hoodlums who kept glancing at them in an uncertain way. So they decided to walk in the middle of the street, without losing sight of these fellows, who in their turn kept their eyes fixed on the students.

Now the tension, permeated as it was by a dense, almost wintry silence, reached its height. Staring each other down, both groups proceeded at a snail's pace toward the goal of the tram stop, which seemed impossibly far away. It was almost as though a magnetic attraction had been set up, and that it was the eyes of the pursuers that prevented greater speed. Or else an unhealthy wish to become better acquainted.

In the end, when the stragglers once more came together in a group at the tram stop, there was a great silent outburst of joy. The challenge had been met; self-control, and perhaps the manifest desire not to sell one's life cheap, had won out over the arrogance of the aggressors. It was a memorable day, one that would have long-lasting repercussions, even if most, not to say all, failed to grasp its deeper meaning.

Next day they learned from Romeo the janitor, and later from other sources, that the supposed attackers were workers from a small factory in the neighborhood, who had themselves heard of the rumored Fascist incursion. So during their lunch break, they had taken up a position along the street where the students would pass, ready to put up their fists, should the need arise. Or maybe just to watch—there was no way of knowing. All the same, for many years there-after, and still today, there are those ready to swear that the great wish of those workers was to beat up the Fascists. To warm up in the cold, and all the more to give vent to their anger.

## II / TRAM 31

The second year of the Jewish School brought changes.

The Villa Celimontana was no longer available, and the school was transferred to the Lungotevere Sanzio, to the building that had once housed the old Israelite Poorhouse. The change was purely formal, but beneath it lay a rather disagreeable truth. If before, by a certain effort of will, the school had been able to claim that it was like any other state institution, now its kinship with the old Jewish quarter of Rome was reinforced, by reason of physical proximity. Stupid bureaucratic complications, such as the expiration of a lease or excessive rent, brought the students back to their earliest origins, which their ancestors had labored so hard to leave behind. The wishes of the rich and powerful had no effect. But meanwhile, as in certain stories by Kafka or Buzzati, which in those very days were beginning to be talked about, the Jews were starting imperceptibly on a downhill path leading no one knew where—perhaps even, in the opinion of the more pessimistic, to the re-establishment of the ghetto. The war had begun, although Italy for the moment was staying out of it.

The class of the previous year was now in the *liceo*. This too was an important change, and it brought others.

Physical training was no longer cultivated with the same enthusiasm as before. The students, having become more mature, now preferred the tram. And this, one might add, is

an important subject that needs to be traced back to its beginnings, both for its implications and for the often considerable consequences that would later develop.

Bicycles having been abandoned, and the tram lines that
most directly connected their respective homes with the
school discontinued, the students agreed that the best transportation, though incomparably slower, was provided by the
Circolare Rossa, the line that made the outer circuit of the city
(it name has since been changed, for it now goes through the
more crowded center). For going home from school, this
choice was no problem: the students simply gathered at the
tram stop to embark on the ride all together, a ride that for
some was more like a journey, but a very enjoyable one for
a complex combination of reasons: it allowed them to go on
with discussions begun in the morning, and encouraged the
development of more or less promising relations with their
female classmates.

This habit met with such favor that it was soon extended to
the morning. And here a small flash of ingenuity was enough
to solve the problem of how to set up a tacit appointment
among students living in the most far-flung quarters of Rome.
Someone simply noticed that in each tram, alongside the
driver, there was a placard with the schedule, and soon the
word went out that No. 31 was the one to take. Around eight
o'clock in the morning, on the Viale della Regina, in Piazza
Quadrata, in Piazza Ungheria, on the Risorgimento bridge,
and along the walls of the Vatican, one could see small groups
of students awaiting the arrival of Tram 31.

Having boarded the tram, you made yourself at home, a
sure sign that the ice had been broken and that all sorts of
new relationships were beginning to be formed. Mutual flir-
tations were struck up between boys showing off their first
long pants, which did not always fit properly, and a few girls
who refused to wear their black smocks outside of school, or

were even bold enough to apply a little lipstick. Such ties were begun and broken with considerable ease: it was indeed a long tram ride, long enough to put the seriousness of these infatuations to the test. Dino felt wittier than ever. Roberto indulged in lengthy arguments, attacking many aspects of high-school wisdom. And all this required a large dose of tolerance from the sleepy morning passengers.

Once you had reached the school, the morning ride had its sequel, pleasant or unpleasant depending on your point of view. It took place during chemistry class, presided over by the domineering Donna Maria, a majestic and imposing teacher who came, as she insistently repeatedly, from the famous Liceo Visconti, the strictest school in Rome. She must have had her informants, for she was always up-to-date on the amorous involvements that had been cemented or dissolved that morning. And it wasn't enough for her to know: she obviously wanted to manipulate and egg on the two parties. "Laura, I see why you didn't do your homework, it's because you've quarreled with Dino." "Vittorio, you're especially distracted this morning. I know why. You've started going steady with Paola again. I'd really like to know what you get out of it." It was obvious what *she* got out of it: an immense, almost indescribable pleasure in stirring up gossip. So immense that a good half of the lesson was sometimes wasted in tittle-tattle, and there was not even time for Donna Maria's dreaded quizzes, which left their mark, especially if the boy was a bit of a skirt-chaser or the girl particularly pretty. Whenever the unfortunate victim's eyes sought help from some printed passage, her intimidating voice would resound: "And stop looking in your book—don't think I don't see you. *Si charta deficit, tota scientia squagliat.*" Can anyone be blamed, under the circumstances, for cunningly bringing up the subject of interrupted romance? It was such an easy game. All you had to say was: "Signorina, have you heard about Vittorio and

poor Paola?" "Why poor? She didn't have to lead him on. And
what's happened that's so tragic? Tell me all about it."

The quiz could be considered over and the danger averted.
The victim had not been sacrificed in vain, for Donna Maria
that morning would no longer mistreat anyone.

Still there was the mystery of where she got her information. Open cases *ad vitandam interrogationem* aside, it was
inconceivable that there would be secret talebearing among
the students. From time to time, on the famous Tram 31, a
teacher might be seen sitting apart in silence, and to judge by
appearances immersed in an important book. But much as
one tried to see a connection, there was no way to imagine
who could have lent himself to being a source of information.

Signorina Lidia, the Greek and Latin teacher, so serious, so
reserved, so quick to blush . . . And anyway wasn't it she who
at all hours kept repeating the warning to "go slow with
etymologies"? Nor could it be Signorina Emma, who taught
mathematics and physics. She was a sort of undisciplined
tomboy, always ready to incite her students not to show too
much respect for the authorities. Once she had even urged
them to strike, which the government at the time considered
a criminal act: it was winter and there was no heat in the
classrooms. "It's your own fault," she had remarked senten-
tiously, "because you act like sheep. Go out on strike and
you'll see how the atmosphere heats up." Such ominous
words, spoken moreover in a clear, plain, basically Tuscan
accent, could not fail to make a great impression. No, Emma
was not the type to get mixed up in Donna Maria's gossip. She
was very young at the time, but you could already see that as
the years went by she would always be the same, neither old
nor young, eternally suspended over the history of the world
like a mathematical equation. Indeed, she was the daughter
of the famous Guido, one of the greatest mathematicians of

modern times, so it might well have been simply a matter of symbolism. Still, come to think of it, a vein of romantic madness dictated her gestures, perhaps derived from the literary talents of her novelist grandfather, Enrico, so persistently did she demand of her students a concrete, physical passion for the study of mathematics, beyond all abstract pedantry. Among the women teachers, there was also Nuccia, with her marvelous blue eyes, which could hardly see what was right in front of her nose. This was enough to absolve her of all suspicion, and one had to take into consideration the fact of her extreme youth—she was only two or three years older than her pupils. This caused her some of the same problems, and she had to be on her guard, since nothing that concerned teachers or students escaped Donna Maria's insatiably curious eyes.

There remained the male teachers. But who would have dared to suspect the Italian teacher, so serious and circumspect, and half asleep on his feet? He was, moreover, an accomplished musician, and spent his nights composing a weighty opera entitled *Inés de Suarez*, which had been commissioned from him by the Chilean government (this Inés would seem to have been a kind of South American Anita Garibaldi). Its composition dragged on for the whole school year, and in the morning the look of its creator clearly showed signs of his sleepless night. He would open a book at random and say through his yawns: "Take a look at this *Orlando Furioso* and see what you can make of it."

The school also had a teacher of religion, since in no way whatsoever was it supposed to differ from the public schools. For some reason or other, they had picked a rabbi who, because of his almost incomprehensible pronunciation of Italian, seldom had occasion to conduct services—as far as Hebrew was concerned, the question was of little importance. Everyone thought him an excellent teacher—he had a great big head, as they liked to say, and certainly it was imposing, majestically bovine—but because of the odd way he had of swallowing his words, he did not succeed in sharing his wisdom with anyone. The students played tricks on him. For example, perhaps taking their inspiration from Edgar Allan Poe's "A Tale of Jerusalem," they found it amusing to put a slice of ham on his desk. But the joke fell flat, because he never noticed anything that happened around him. And even had he seen something, his reaction would probably have been incomprehensible to everyone. Just as one can be sure that he would not have heard a single word uttered by his young students. He was a man completely isolated in his inner sphere. With time and the growth of intellectual experience, someone suggested that the religion teacher, familiar as he was with the *Cabala* and the *Zohar*, had fulfilled the dream of mystical suspension above this harsh and disappointing world. Not everyone, however, accepted this explanation. Some were more inclined to link such stubborn concentration with anticipation of the next meal: it was not angelic *sephiroth* that had danced before those dreamy, watery eyes, but delicious beefsteaks and plates of steaming noodles.

Thus, as was to be expected, the search by the boys and girls always led the dynamics of their little world back to an elementary dualism, the clash between the only two forces that were visibly contending for control over base matter, namely the boys and girls themselves.

Who indeed was Donna Maria's true adversary, the declared enemy of her Aristotelian pedantry, the blasphemous belittler of the tradition that held sway at the Liceo Visconti? Who was the tireless corrupter of hapless youth, hurling corrosive ridicule at "comprehensive examinations on the subjects studied during the year" and the finicky gradation of marks, from 5-plus to 6-minus-minus? Who was the subverter of the tried and true methods used by generations of cautious school superintendents? Who was the new Socrates, who in Donna Maria's mind lacked only an Athens that would rival that ancient one and hand him a brimming cup of hemlock?

The new Socrates came from Ancona. But his ancestry went back much further, to the far north of Italy, the Piedmont of the Savoys, a region much more remote from the South than would appear from the map. One should not forget, since it's an important element, that Donna Maria spoke with a strong Neapolitan accent. And she was unaware, poor woman, that in the city of her studies, this young Socrates had been a pupil of one of the staunchest enemies of the pedantic tradition in Italian education—Augusto Monti, whose legend, for better or worse, was to have lasting effects.

The students were eager to finish the *ginnasio* and be admitted to the *liceo*, where Monferini taught. He cared little about his unusual popularity—or at least so he pretended. But there was an obvious touch of vanity in his great bushy mop of disheveled, slightly graying hair, dividing at the top into two lesser bushes. Underneath were two sharp pinpoints in place of eyes, and a mouth that was always ready to widen in a smirk or an outburst of laughter. To make Donna Maria furious, one had only to remind her that he was very skillful in imitating an orangutan, the grotesque gait and facial expressions that make it a caricature of man. But he was not her only opponent.

The other teacher of history and philosophy, whose job it was to supervise candidates for the Normal School, was an austere admirer of Mazzini, and resembled Giuseppe Verdi in every way, including, it was whispered, his scant propensity for personal hygiene. He loved to transform the classrooms into so many temples, and his own lectures into moving orations culminating in subdued and dignified tears, whereupon he would conclude with a ringing quotation from

Mazzini's *Doveri dell'uomo*. The French teacher, a skinny little woman as sassy and disrespectful as a Tuscan serving wench, once threw open the door in the middle of his lecture-oration, and said in a shrill voice: "Bring your dictionaries tomorrow, boys and girls!" He blasted her with a look, observed a few moments of reinvigorating silence, and then with a visible effort took up the thread of his peroration. Again the door flew open, and the same petulant voice rang out: "I've changed my mind, boys and girls. No classwork, so don't bring your dictionaries." At this point came an explosion. Verdi's moustache and beard entered into conflict with Mazzini's acidity, while a savage yell sprang from the depths of the rights of man. The culprit was followed into the teachers' room, and there dramatically confronted with the supreme wisdom: "Signorina, don't you know there's a great difference between you and me?" The wretched woman stared back at him, and replied, in her incurably shrill voice: "I'm a big girl now, Professor, and I know the difference."

The story of this incident made the rounds of the school, and there could be no doubt as to who had spread it. This conclusion only helped to increase the students' curiosity about meeting Monferini. And anyway it was not something that could be postponed: it was written in the laws of the school that even the boys and girls in the *ginnasio* must eventually make his acquaintance.

Instead, the first lesson turned out to be more ordinary than anyone would have thought. The bushy head made its appearance, the thin body settled itself and disappeared behind the desk. Without even a preamble, the lecture on the pre-Socratic philosophers began, in terms that could not have been more irritating and boring. A lesson like so many others.

The only departure from routine was when Romeo the janitor came to call Monferini to the principal's office. He was out of the room for quite a while. As often happens in such circumstances, the silence that followed his exit turned into a murmur, then into excitement, and then into an unrestrained uproar. For all of Romeo's gesticulating, he was unsuccessful in warning the students that the teacher was on his way back.

By the time this reality became clear, it was too late for order to be restored. Professor Monferini was already seated at his desk. He gazed around with eyes more curious than suspicious, and went on with his lecture.

The bell rang, but he showed no signs of having heard it. He went on expatiating on Protagoras and Anaximander, in the same low, calm tone of voice, while the students, feeling understandably guilty, paid strict attention, quite out of proportion to the boring subject. So out of proportion that at a certain point Monferini could no longer go on pretending. He stood up and asked the whole class: "Can you possibly all be so interested in the string of nonsense I've been reeling off for over half an hour? Is no one brave enough to tell me that the bell rang some time ago?"

There followed an awestruck, faltering silence, which no one seemed able to break.

"You," Monferini went on, having meanwhile seated himself on a corner of the desk, as was his habit when in a good mood, "you find yourselves in a special situation, attending a school somewhat different from all the others. Your history and philosophy teacher, who happens to be myself, must also act as assistant principal, for reasons I won't go into. It's neither your fault nor mine. Many things happen in life that we don't much care for, but which we can't get out of. These situations, and still more serious ones, like the racial laws that have brought you to this classroom, can't be helped, at least for the moment. We must face up to them seriously, and even with a positive attitude—like men, but truly like men. I have

to count on you, not as children whose caprices and imper-
tinence can be forgiven, but as adults, in whom one can have
complete trust. I honestly can't tell whether you're mature
enough. But I have no other choice, and since at first sight
you look like you're normally intelligent, I don't see why you
shouldn't behave like mature and civilized human beings. If
then this turns out to be impossible for you, so much the
worse for me, but above all so much the worse for you."

He looked pensive, as though following a train of thought
that combined tough questions of both a pragmatic and moral
kind.

"Correction," he said. "So much the worse for me. Because
it'll make me late for lunch, as it has today. I don't know about
you, but when this moment comes, I'm starving."

And he broke out in an unexpected guffaw, which after a
moment of confusion, but only a moment, communicated
itself to all the students, who were already thronging around
their teacher, and despite the late hour no longer wished to
get away.

Nor did he, for his part, remember that he was hungry. He
joked good-naturedly, and exchanged wisecracks about the
abstruseness of the subject matter. He only limited himself to
warning: "Have a little patience, before you pass judgment."
But the students had already passed judgment, and none of
them would ever retract it: a man like Monferini, teacher and
friend, always, or almost always, spoke his mind, no matter
who was present. And—something even more to be prized—
what he said never aroused resentment in anyone, neither in
the speaker, nor in whoever was the object, not to mention in
the others, who formed a circle around him wishing to learn.

## III / THE SACRED ENCLOSURE

It was a strange phenomenon. New friendships were being formed, and with each passing day a cheerful, human atmosphere was being created. But this remained within the tiny circle of the state-controlled Jewish School. Outside, in public, the climate was becoming increasingly tense. Heavy clouds kept gathering, and there was a feeling that something very unpleasant was about to happen.

Some had had an inkling that it would take a war to unravel all the knots in which the country was ensnared. But this had been a vague notion, almost aesthetic in nature, and in any case very far from any precise idea of what was to be the reality of the war. At the age of fifteen one may think of war as a swift, even heroic solution to certain problems. That's human and understandable. But once you begin to realize that it is in man's power to wish for war and unleash it, but certainly not to end it by a simple act of will—when your eyes are opened to the revelation of what a slow, exhausting agony war is— you see it in a different light. You are aware of its approach, but no longer dare to open your heart to expectations. You simply hold your breath, hoping the tempest will pass and do as little damage as possible, at least in the circle of your nearest and dearest. Until later, much later, you realize that man is nothing but a straw at the mercy of a perpetual war, in a world constantly boiling, where anything can happen at any moment, beyond our will and capacity to resist. This is neither good nor evil; it is simply life, which always contains, by the external law of its own nature, its other complementary and indistinguishable element—what we call death. But if we come to be aware at all of this simple truth, so contrary to our way of seeing things, it is only much later.

When danger looms, each of us inevitably thinks first of his own safety. But an obscure premonition often makes us aware that safety can lie only in the union of many. Probably there are very few who, at the approach of the most violent blasts, withdraw from and flee the company of others. In most, for reasons deeply buried in the phylogenetic history of this animal species, the herd instinct re-emerges.

The students thought it was their romantic crushes, their budding friendships, and the profound influence exerted by Monferini's words that had brought them closer together outside of school hours. All these reasons existed, of course, but there was something else. It was hard to put your finger on it.

Meanwhile they were no longer ashamed of being Jews. Even those—and this perhaps means most—who came from families with the secular traditions of the Risorgimento, thus with a distinct vein of anticlericalism that was naturally also directed against the Jewish religion, began to feel a strange, unmotivated pride in being Jews. And it was no longer, as it had been at first, that peculiar masochistic pride in belonging to a band of reprobates. It was something more, but still impossible to define.

In imitation of some of the adults in their respective families, they did their utmost to trace titles of nobility, presumed rather than genuine, which chiefly meant listing, in a confused hodgepodge, the great men who had brought honor to the race: Einstein, Freud, Spinoza, Mendelssohn (the composer, a convert to Christianity, while no mention was made of his grandfather, the great apostle of the Jewish Enlightenment), and then Moses, Jesus of Nazareth, and a certain General Pugliese, of the Corps of Engineers, of whom it was said that Mussolini, despite all the racial laws, was unable to do without. To end with the greatest of all, the famous actor Charlie Chaplin. By the way, could one really be sure that Chaplin was a Jew? Some swore to it, as though they'd been present at the circumcision ceremony. Others weren't all that sure. Even today, in certain circles, the doubt lingers.

More serious research, such as befitted a group of *liceo* students, began to be conducted in the direction of good books. But in this field their friend Monferini confessed that he couldn't be of much help. Not even he understood on what grounds the Fascist government had classified him as a Jew. With some difficulty, they got hold of a Bible, since it wasn't easy, in that benighted Italy, to avail oneself of the pleasure of reading it. But for most it turned out to be an abstruse book, hard to decipher, so discouragingly remote that it might just as well have been about Maya civilization or the customs of ancient Tibetan tribes.

They fell back on Israel Zangwill, who if nothing else was a pleasant writer. They knew nothing about him, and did not even suspect that he had played a part in the Zionist movement, first alongside Herzl, and later in open conflict with him. But his *Italian Fantasies*, discovered on some dusty bookshelf, spoke a strikingly florid language, something between the aestheticism of d'Annunzio and a certain genial humanitarianism, thus creating a synthesis, as ideal as it was fictitious, between two opposed requirements and cultures. It was more invigorating to read his best short novel *King of the Schnorrers*, which through its restrained humor exalts the stereotype of the presumptuous, bragging, shyster Jew who has been the object of an age-old tradition of malicious caricature. The device consisted in turning the traditional perspective on its head, and converting what habitually had been

considered worthy only of contempt into something praise-
worthy and even agreeable.

It's hard to say if the decision taken by the students was a
remote consequence of such reading. But the fact is that at a
certain moment many resolved to go to the Temple on Friday
evening.

Rome's main synagogue is one of the ugliest buildings
erected since the liberation of the Risorgimento. It was built
on the site of the five ancient Scholae much admired by
Gregorovius. Incredibly small, grouped in a single crumbling
building, each had practiced the rite of its original congregation: Sicilian, Aragonese, Catalan, Castilian, and of course
Italian. Over the centuries, the remains of nearby Roman
temples, Corinthian columns and architraves, had piled up
there; then precious fabrics, left over from the wedding cer-
emonies of Roman noblewomen and adapted for sacred use;
and objects of chiseled and embossed silver, fruit of the skill
of neighboring craftsmen, in the days when they were all
called masters of the art, though they certainly were not to be
compared with a Benvenuto Cellini. Nevertheless, the objects
that emerged from their workshops were not unbecoming,
whatever the material that the customer had asked for.

Everything, or almost everything, had been swept away by
the slum-clearing pickaxe at the end of the century. No question but it was a necessary operation. Fetid alleyways, ancient
breeding grounds of infection, disappeared, as did tottering
structures whose owners were unable to provide any main-
tenance, since the *ius gazagà*, the law of perpetual tenancy
granted by papal charity to the unfortunate Jews of the Roman ghetto, had not allowed any rent increases for centuries;
nor could the overwhelming majority of tenants—tailors,
seamstresses, ragpickers, small junk dealers—have been able
to afford such increases. Winding paths, which had been
flooded by the churning waters of the Tiber and the overflow

from nearby sewers during periods of heavy rain, likewise disappeared, as did the five Scholae, though no one paid attention or raised a protest. Nothing is left but Gregorovius's description of them and a few faded photographs in the museum of the Palazzo Braschi.

The Jews of Rome held their heads high, having achieved a civic dignity that they had despaired of ever regaining. Now they cared much less about being in a synagogue, the only place, in times of supreme affliction, that had allowed them to feel they were their own masters, albeit under the frowning gaze of the God they shared with the Christians. New attractions now lay open before them, exciting adventures with the flavor of the unknown, and perhaps of wealth and fame: careers in the magistracy, the army, the fine arts, the professions, the government. But the norms of the beautiful and happy society that they were being summoned to enter required a Temple, not a Schola, and not even a Synagogue, for the observance of certain supreme moments of existence: births, weddings, deaths. Not so much for prayer, and still less for the study of the age-old wisdom, which had been the original function of these places, Synagogue as well as Schola, unwitting translations of the traditional terms *Beth ha-Keneseth* (House of the Community) and *Beth ha-Midrash* (House of Study).

They accordingly embarked on an ambitious project, intended to symbolize a considerable number of concepts. The new Israelite Temple—the word "Jewish" being rather unpopular—was planned chiefly as a "sacred enclosure," in the idiom dear to generations of presidents and councillors of the Community. And also a Temple of Liberty—restored liberty—and Reason, with unconscious Masonic overtones, as expressed in the severe and functional lines, barely softened, particularly in the interior, by some touching highlights of Art Nouveau. One was also supposed to see a reference, as moving as it was naive, and completely out of keeping with the surroundings, to the Assyro-Babylonian origins of the patriarch Abraham, who was not, and could not have been, merely a wretched Bedouin. The hope was to achieve a tone of restrained richness, one that would not offend the discretion of the elderly, while at the same time comparing favorably with nearby Christian churches.

All these complicated problems were handled by the Community's president, the popular lawyer Angelino Sereni, a visitor to the Royal Palace but who, like most of his contemporaries, had not forgotten the rules of shrewd management—or miserliness, as his anti-Semitic detractors might have said. In any case, he could draw comfort from the example set by the king himself, the young Victor Emmanuel, a true Savoyard mountaineer almost as tight-fisted as a Jew, for different historical reasons but with a common memory of adversity in more or less remote times.

Angelo Sereni had a million lire at his disposal for the construction of the Temple, a sum that seemed fabulous in most people's eyes but certainly was not. His secret pride, his unconfessed ambition, was to complete the job for less, if only a little less, than that ideal goal; were he to go beyond it, he would be exposed to everlasting shame. And he succeeded, incredible as it may seem to us who have witnessed the extravagance of many modern administrators, especially of public works. He succeeded albeit at the cost of some unappealing subterfuges, like the majestic columns that are marble only halfway up, and then become stucco, duly reinforced, all the way to the highest vault. But, to be fair, who would ever notice it at that height?

There's no way of knowing whether Victor Emmanuel, king by the grace of God and the will of the Italian nation, noticed it during his memorable visit to the Temple, on July 2, 1904, twenty-five days before the official opening. But one can imagine he did, since he had a sharp and ravening eye, examine everything minutely in accordance with his fussy nature, and demand from his deferential escorts, as we read in a newspaper account of the time, "an explanation of every single thing, while expressing satisfaction and praise to everyone."

> After visiting the central hall of the Temple, where he had the opportunity to admire the high cupola surmounting it, His Majesty proceeded to the large Council Room, where he was pleased to sign the special Album that will be jealously preserved as a record of his august visit. He thereupon ascended to the women's gallery, from there admiring the painted decorations of the cupola and walls of the Temple, and congratulating the painters Brugnoli and Bruschi, who had executed them. . . .
>
> To demonstrate his great satisfaction with his visit to the grandiose edifice, without doubt worthy of both Roman Jewry and the entire city, His Majesty the King was pleased to name by his own initiative President Sereni and the architects Armanni and Costa Officers of the Crown of Italy, and to accompany these decorations with highly complimentary letters.

This may not seem like much, given the inflated notions of that generation's grandchildren. But, as we have seen, Victor Emmanuel and Angelo Sereni understood each other well, and had the same cautious, penny-pinching mentality. For men of their stamp, one glance was enough to formulate the same harmonious thought: is the reward appropriate to the circumstances and expense; if not, what should we do on future occasions? There is still no way of knowing whether the king, on affixing his signature to the racial laws thirty-four years later, had any recollection of that memorable day and looked around to see if he still had more decorations to bestow.

It was in the intellectual field that no heed was paid to expense: the composition of songs in praise of the happy event, and admonitory inscriptions posted in every corner of the Temple. If proof of this is needed, one has only to transcribe the hymn, composed in Hebrew and Italian, "in honor of the Lord, on the day of the consecration of the new Israelite Temple of Rome by the Grand Rabbi Vittorio Castiglioni." It contains everything, from the historical and ideological standpoint, making it worth reading and pondering even today, without going into the question of poetic values, which may be there but have so far gone unnoticed.

> Lord, Thy power defies description
> Thy mercies to Thy chosen band,
> Thy good counsel and prescriptions
> Are loftier than we understand.
>
> In this great Eternal City
> We have borne a heavy load;
> Now in brotherhood and pity,
> We build Thee a new abode.
>
> From Thy throne in Heaven above,
> Guard this House from evil days,
> God of pardon and of love,
> Accept Thy people's ardent gift,
> As they bow before this altar,
> The whole world with them uplift.

What a pity that the great Verdi had died barely three years before! Surely, with his deep convictions, he would not have scorned to set it to music, and as for the words, he had put up with much worse from his librettists. Perhaps he would not

even have asked too high a fee from the president of the
Community—although, being a peasant by origin, and by his
own admission remaining such to the end of his days, he too
knew the value of money. He would have set it to music and
doubtless have come up with something imperishable.

So the Jews of Rome got their Temple, but once the intoxication of the solemn celebration had worn off, they felt no
urge to attend it. The old people, still tied to their memories
of the ghetto, which, strange as it may seem, turned into great
nostalgia, mourned the mild atmosphere of the Scholae,
where from their fathers' lips they had learned to intone
*Shema Israel*, *Adon Olam*, and *Yigdal Elohim hay*.* Their
sons, now officers, magistrates, and teachers, or else wholesale merchants whose outlook was bourgeois, were ashamed
to repeat these dirges, whose meaning they did not
understand—but then neither did their parents. The leaders
of the Community rushed to the rescue. They modified the
garb of the officiants to make them look more like priests.
They introduced new melodies for traditional texts, commis-
sioning them from a fashionable composer, which to them
meant some modest follower of Mercadante and Bellini. They
even bore the extravagant cost of an organ, so that the Temple would no longer have any reason to envy a Christian
church. But parents continued to drag themselves there re-

---

* The first of these traditional chants is connected with the solemn
declaration of faith of the Jewish people: "Hear, O Israel, the Lord
our God, the Lord is one" (cf. Deuteronomy 6:4, 5-9, as well as
Numbers 15:37-41). The second, "Lord of the world," bears witness
to divine omnipotence; while the third, by the philosopher Moses
Maimonides, who lived in Spain during the period of Muslim dom-
ination, begins with the words "I believe in the living God," and
continues by listing the thirteen articles of the Jewish faith, as they
developed over centuries of theological debate, in contrast to the
relative vagueness of biblical statements.

luctantly, chiefly for the peace of their souls, and their children kept up their habit of absence and indifference.

The one exception was for Yom Kippur, the solemn day of fasting and atonement. People began talking about it a month beforehand, at the end of summer vacation, as an impending, unavoidable nuisance. But it was the last show of attachment demanded by the elders and the rabbi, a day of total concentration, before resuming the pace of one's usual labors, and an opportunity to rediscover later, with the old folks around the family table in the evening, a sense of patriarchal customs that had now been hopelessly lost.

For the younger generation the day was a nightmare. Already that incomprehensible business of fasting for twenty-five hours in a row, which few people dreamed of imposing by coercion, but all invoked as an act of social decorum and a manifestation of pride to flaunt at the "others," those credulous and bigoted Catholics, was enough to induce a bad mood. Which only grew as you approached the sacred enclosure and saw the crowd that began arriving in the late afternoon between five and six. It was truly an imposing throng, and included the prosperous middle class, which had left the ghetto behind, and the subproletariat, still tied to the old quarter out of work habits or simple inertia: an incredible contrast of attitudes, clothing, and behavior. The carabinieri, in dress uniform, did their best to control the crowd, but were themselves a cause of confusion, inspiring the same comment year after year: "For our holy Yom Kippur they even call out the carabinieri!"

This was just a prelude to the frightful madhouse, the pushing and shoving, and combination of odors that filled the Temple, that solid structure designed by the architects Costa and Armanni. The children, flung this way and that, searched anxiously for their fathers and grandfathers, but with no hope of succeeding since all the men looked alike under the unusual covering of their silk prayer shawls, which had been taken out of the bottom of a drawer for that one day. To follow the progress of the ceremony was out of the question, with the steadily increasing crowd waving its arms and calling out; one could just barely hear the nasal sing-song of someone in the distance, or, more likely, nearby but exhausted from his prolonged fast.

The crowning moment, that of the solemn blessing, was drawing near. The cries and shoving increased, as many people rushed outside to summon their scattered relatives and to bring babies inside who had so far been kept out of range of all the confusion. Everyone gathered under the prayer shawl of his father, who spread his arms in a vain attempt to touch each one's head. The tallest were obliged to keep their heads low, until the discomfort and pain of this position became unbearable. The liveliest consoled themselves by exchanging silly jokes. But there was always a father or uncle to admonish them, half playfully, half sternly, "Be serious and behave yourselves. At least on this day. Try to remember all your sins. And repent, if you can."

Finally something like silence was established, as compared to the preceding din. A voice, still faint but of a different timbre, raised falteringly in the air incomprehensible words or sounds that created a peculiar kind of magic. And the magic soon ended in the blurting of raucous calls, a kind of savage bellowing, at the same time fearful and ridiculous: it was the *shofar* of the holy pastoral ancestors, the ram's horn that in the desert must truly have sounded like the thundering voice of the Holy One who is, was, and will be the Lord of Hosts, the Lord of his proud and stubborn servant Israel.

This sound, echoing a few meters from the automobile traffic and the clanking trams, amid the blaring of radios and the lazy flow of the Tiber, was the signal of final liberation. Hearty handshakes and greetings were dispensed to all and

sundry: acquaintances, street vendors, opponents in countless arguments, perfect strangers, and the dumbfounded carabiniere. Then everyone rushed home, eager to end the fast.

It was the last ceremony in that exhausting day, and it too
was heavy, but rather more agreeable. Custom required that
the dishes served, once traditional and today almost forgotten, be prepared the day before. Broth, hastily reheated in
the time it took to get home from the sacred enclosure, then
mullet drenched in vinegar with raisins and pine nuts,
chicken in aspic (the pride of surviving grandmothers), and
pickled zucchini, fried and then marinated again in sharp
vinegar. And, finally, certain sweets of dubious taste, also
traditional but no longer made at home, and which had to be
purchased in some miserable little bakery known only to the
old folks: *straccaganasse*, *ginetti*, tarts, and other such deli-
cacies. Everybody was hungry, and that was enough to make
them happy. Yom Kippur was now behind them. The next
one was still a year away.

This long preamble has been needed to explain the difficult psychological obstacles that the students had to overcome in order to cross the threshold of the sacred enclosure,
whether on an ordinary day, a Friday evening, or a Saturday
morning. But at fifteen or sixteen years of age, one has the
strength and stubbornness to carry out such decisions. Usually the first cigarette tastes awful, and yet it is just at the age
of fifteen or sixteen that one learns to smoke. And then there
was Giorgio to encourage and urge on the more reluctant—
Giorgio, who had already undertaken on his own to investigate the sources of Judaism, and found an atmosphere at
home that was still conducive to a certain number of customs
and traditions.

One Friday evening a little group of five or six gathered at
the Temple. It was winter, and the sun was about to set. The
service would shortly begin.

The boys filed silently into the already dark interior, and, led by Giorgio, reached the front benches, all of which were empty. They hesitated whether to sit down, since no one had given them permission. But a broad sign from Giorgio settled it, and sitting down, they waited for something to happen.

Each bench bore a brass plate engraved with the name, complete with titles, of some member of the Community. This already made the boys feel uneasy. But it was still more unpleasant to feel themselves the object of cruel and inquiring stares by the few regular worshippers in the Temple. Old men with suspicious eyes and hooked noses seemed to be relentlessly weighing the significance of their presence. Some were exchanging impressions, doubtless unfavorable. The light, produced as it was by a few low-watt bulbs, was uncertain. Above, behind a balustrade, two shabbily dressed men went back and forth, engaged in some unimportant matter.

All of a sudden, one of them leaned over the balustrade and spoke in a low voice to one of the regular worshippers in the Temple. He nodded his head and disappeared behind a side column, as though going backstage. He soon came back, transformed in bearing and costume. He now wore a dignified tailcoat and had adorned his chest with a mysterious silver medallion, suspended from his shoulders by a chain. On it were engraved three Hebrew letters, whose meaning was unknown to the students. On his head he had placed a slightly shabby top hat. The boys would certainly have laughed had they not realized that this individual was coming in their direction.

The man took a few steps forward, beyond the row of benches where the boys were sitting. Here he stopped, leaned down, and whispered in each one's ear: "Your head, you have to cover your head, here are some little caps." And to each he handed a black skullcap, which was accepted and examined with the greatest mistrust.

It ought to be mentioned that Giorgio had recalled beforehand that to enter the Jewish Temple you had to wear something on your head. He had come supplied with an old-fashioned dark blue beret, which had made the others laugh. All had been in agreement in refusing to submit to this ridiculous requirement. They considered themselves free men, studying philosophy with Professor Monferini as their teacher, and though they still hadn't got beyond Plato and Aristotle, they were already looking forward to the free and independent Benedict Spinoza, and still further to the immortal principles of the French Revolution. But now they were fingering these little black skullcaps, which didn't look all that clean, and were unable to come to a decision. But by the time the man in the top hat had come back and handed each a small prayer book, which had obviously endured the greasy thumbs of several generations, each one had resolved his doubts. The skullcaps were in place, and without realizing it, the century's free children had been transformed, in the eyes of anyone observing and judging them, into respectable Jews.

The second layman, who had been walking back and forth on the other side of the balustrade, reappeared robed in a long black cassock, his head covered with an Anglo-Saxon university mortarboard. He moved to the center, turning his back on the others, and without warning began grinding out on his own a monotonous dirge, occasionally interrupted by variations in a nasal key. Almost immediately a contest developed, between those up above and those below, as to who was going faster; but the latter, being more numerous, always got ahead of the official cantor, who in any case paid little attention to this affront. From time to time, one of the old men would stand up and utter in a loud voice a sentence punctuated by the word *barukh* ("blessed be ..."), a recurrent invocation in many Jewish prayers, and then sit down again, satisfied to see that the others, beaten to the punch, only now were beginning to do likewise.

All this standing up and sitting down constituted a serious problem. The boys peered anxiously around, trying to guess the moment at which the rite prescribed this act of devotion, and now quite ready to imitate it. But they failed to discern any sign whatsoever indicating the moment's arrival. It could only be explained by the wish felt by each old man to get there before the others, and thus corner all the divine favor for himself. Indeed, the act of standing up was almost always followed by deep prostrations, increasingly accentuated, so that the Almighty would be able to see who was manifesting the most zeal.

After this hectic phase came the final moment, which consisted in the elevation of a chalice and the declamation of some verses of benediction, these last being pronounced in a more distinct voice. Immediately thereafter all the worshippers, including the cantor, left in the same hurry, heads bowed and without uttering a word.

The boys looked at each other in silence, afraid to make any comments. The man in the top hat stared at them grimly, making it plain that once the service was over, it was time to vacate the sacred enclosure.

When they reached the exit, Giorgio broke the silence. "The Friday evening service," he said, "has changed with time. You can see why: the way we live, it's hard to interrupt whatever we're doing. It's unfortunate, but that's how things are today. But the really important service is the one on Saturday, and it's just as alive as in the past."

He said nothing more, fearful of pressing them too hard. And no one paid much attention to his words, which remained hanging there in mid-air, between the Palazzo Cenci and the eddies of the Tiber, in the heart of ancient, skeptical Rome. And it flowed placidly, the Tiber, now finally tamed, after the floods of the Middle Ages, by the industrious sons of Reason, whose leader was the hero Garibaldi, a fighter in this holy battle as well. The Tiber calls to mind many legends, like the one of the Abbasid Arabs, who described it as glittering with sheets of bronze; and many suggestive sights, as when during winter sunsets, flames from the overhanging clouds seem, for no more than a moment, to come down and touch the water. But that is pure illusion, and no one believes in legends any more, especially of those remote, unknown beings, the Arabs. Who, in our times, would think it possible for there to be a flood, not to mention a fire on the Tiber?

## IV / LEKHAH DODI

It's hard to remember, after all this time, exactly when this incredible episode took place. But take place it did. One Saturday morning, a week or a month later, the boys once more set foot in the Temple.

It was a period of intense discussions of various kinds, both political and conceptual. As they pursued their studies, they increasingly immersed themselves in remote worlds, which appeared infinitely better than the present one—the effect, as we know, of distance. At their side stood an invaluable, irreplaceable friend, who had the rare capacity to bring ancient problems back to life in all their complexity, without bothering to make the students memorize a lot of dry facts, the method so dear to pedants of the old school. With Monferini, to speak of Athens or Rome meant taking up an unsuspected host of questions. A lecture on Aristotle might involve the technical aspects of harnessing animals, the concept of slavery or that of friendship, methods of deterrence and punishment. Ancient Rome was depicted as a complicated center of rational and oppressive exploitation; the road-building Romans were revealed to be geniuses of state organization, the inventors of a shrewd and efficent bureaucracy. Everything came to seem logical and connected, even the emotional suicide Cato, the skeptical Horace, and the lascivious Catullus. Sometimes, indeed often, discoveries about ancient worlds shed unexpected light on the agonizing problems of the modern world. This kind of approach and study might also justify an effort to trace the origins of the ancient Hebrews. It was one more reason, to be added to the other, largely irrational ones that had cropped up.

During the Saturday service, the Temple turned out to be more crowded than on the previous occasion. The individuals were fundamentally the same—direct descendants, in their physiognomies and expressions, of the followers of the great Manasse Bueno Barzilai Azevedo da Costa, king of beggars and a first-class scrounger. It was even possible to recognize on the faces of some the lineaments of their remote Spanish descent. And on Saturday morning they were there in large numbers, representing in the end an outstanding segment of the dispersed Jewish people.

They all wore white prayer shawls, and one could see how this gave them that generally noble and regal appearance noted by Gregorovius. The rabbi, seated behind the balustrade on a marble dais, also looked majestic, with his stony, motionless face, whose most expressive feature was the square-cut gray beard. His gaze, ignoring the confusion of the noisy crowd, was fixed on certain cabalistic symbols, the mysterious cryptograms in which the terrifying power of the Holy Name is contained.

But as the morning service progressed, it was no less disappointing than the one on Friday evening. The usual incomprehensible dirges—incomprehensible not only to the boys, but obviously to most of these devout Jews as well—the aforementioned alternation between standing up and sitting down, and the deep prostrations.

At a certain moment, the Ark was opened. Heads were bowed more than ever, and eyes again covered by silk prayer shawls. But the boys, except for Giorgio, who was also displaying his devotion, saw the man in the top hat—the *shammash*, as the silver medallion on his chest indicated, that is to say a mere sexton—pull a cord to open a purple drape, just like a theater curtain. Disclosed to view were five or six bundles of material, topped by peculiar crowns. The same number of volunteers stood ready; they lifted the bundles with supreme care and formed a line, headed by the rabbi.

The procession set off on its way. It was preceded by a boy, who carried a small, sharp, silver object terminating in a tiny hand: the pointer with which the reader would follow the lines of the sacred text. Then came the rabbi, ever more imposing, and then the other devotees, each of whom, with a great show of piety, carried the sacred burden: a scroll of the Law, wound on two cylindrical sticks, and covered with a precious, brightly colored fabric, very beautiful to look at. A silver crown stood out on the cloth as well, while at the ends of the wooden rods were two small turrets, also of silver, in different and unusual shapes, some of them tinkling with little bells.

The procession, very slowly and amid chanting, proceeded to make the circuit of the Temple. As the scrolls passed, the worshippers prostrated themselves still more. Many, a great many, reached out to touch the edge of the cloth, then brought their hands to their eyes and to their lips in a kiss. The circuit completed, the procession reascended the stairs, and the holy scriptures were arranged on either side of the officiant, except one, which was placed open in front of him. He then began the reading of the weekly portion of the biblical text.

The reading consisted in this: one of the aspirants stepped forward, and stammering the Hebrew words put in his mouth by the officiant, uttered a blessing. The officiant responded in the prescribed manner, without failing to announce, but in good Italian, the sum that the volunteer was offering for the honor of the reading. This reading then, in the classical language of King David and the Prophets, was performed by the officiant, and it could not have been otherwise. Meanwhile, the overall commotion increased. The only moment that a circumspect silence occurred was when the inevitable collection was taken up: ten lire, or fifty, or two hundred, for the Charity Fund, to be put at the disposal of the Chief Rabbi, for the School, for the Hospital.

Outside, Giorgio became the center of another scene of embarrassment and misunderstanding. But this time he was more embarrassed than his silent accusers. He was moved to make a silly suggestion, if only to break the surface of the ice before it got any thicker. "Let's go say hello to the rabbi, over on the side of the choir."

If this could help to overcome his dismay and straighten out his ideas, no one cared to raise objections. But the rabbi had already left in a great hurry, taking only the time to remove his robe.

In a narrow passage in the rear of the Temple, some members of the choir, of various ages, still lingered.

"I'd like to introduce Gino," said Giorgio, in a deliberately casual tone. "He's just been appointed choir director."

An unusually tall young man, thin as a Don Quixote who has not yet reached the age of thirty, bowed to the newcomers with an amused, infinitely cryptic smile.

"To be the director of the Temple choir is a very honorable post, out of proportion to my qualifications and my age. Let me introduce you to the more important members, in here."

There were, in his opinion, several of them. Biscotto, the tenor soloist, was a local Othello, with dark skin and bloodshot eyes, under thick, kinky, silver hair: an Othello who having survived the murder of his wife, was now dedicated to works of piety. But he was also a factotum of the ghetto, one who knew all there was to know about his coreligionists—to the point that they came to him, in preference to the banks, to obtain reliable information on property and inheritance. Furthermore, he was an able marriage broker.

Uncle Marco, as he was called by all the other choristers, was a middle-aged gentleman wearing a dignified homburg. He took his leave almost immediately, sparing the boys considerable discomfiture. It was so obvious he belonged to the tumultuous world of business, you could only wonder why he bothered with the choir.

The organist was a little old man with a sweet, dreamy expression. His head bowed over the keyboard, he looked as though he were taking a nap, while instead he was following some celestial melody, as shown by the movement of his shoes on the pedals. Or else this was his habit, the result of repeated gestures. He was a Christian, of course, otherwise he would not have been able to perform his task on Saturday. But over the years he had become such a participant in the life of the Community that he had assimilated the ways, and even the physiognomy, of the inhabitants of the ghetto. Who knows if he might not have had a great wish to convert, thus completing this long spiritual journey. But he couldn't, since by becoming a Jew he would have lost his job. Just as the congregation would have gained a Jew but lost its organist.

"This," said Gino, with a smile that disclosed his prominent teeth, "is a terrific observation post. From back here you can follow the service in a completely different way."

He realized that he had aroused the curiosity of his listeners, and went on with a conspiratorial smile mingling irony, sympathy, and understanding.

"Do you know what the rabbi was thinking today? Too bad, but I can't tell you. It's a professional secret."

It was a rather shameless trick to excite the curiosity of his listeners. But the musician Gino must have been very fond of this kind of suspense.

"I got a good look at what he was holding between the

pages of his book. You'd never believe it! And the president of the Community, you've no idea what he's been thinking about."

There was no way to get him to reveal what the rabbi was thinking. Now he had switched to the president's concerns.

"This much I can tell anyone, because you could see it in his eyes. He was thinking about the Community budget and how to have more kinds of weddings."

The boys stared at him in amazement, but this, of course, was part of Gino's fun.

"We already have three categories of weddings, first, second, and third, the same as for funerals. But now he's thought up some ingenious ways to differentiate the first: with a carpet, with flowers, with a white drapery in front of the *hekhal*, with organ alone, with organ and chorus, with organ, chorus, and violin. By the way, I forgot to introduce you to Sergio, our young violinist. He's very young and shy, he still hasn't finished the Conservatory. Anyway, brides always ask for the same pieces: Mendelssohn's Wedding March and Handel's Largo. But the one they want most is Gounod's Ave Maria."

"The Ave Maria?"

"It always causes an argument. But it's played by a solo violin, you don't get the words."

Such situations amused Maestro Gino tremendously. There was no way of telling whether they were true or if he was making them up.

"And now, if you don't mind, I must say goodbye. My work is waiting."

"Are you going to the Conservatory?"

"I wish I were! I'm off to sell straw handbags. I've got a family and need to earn money. And music, as everyone knows. . ."

He went away, stooping slightly, perhaps from a wish to minimize his excessive height. Even his overcoat looked too small for him, since he had to pull up the collar to cover his nose, which was somewhat red from the winter cold.

A few days later, several students met again at Giorgio's house. He was always hospitable, and had an older brother, an engineer, who didn't mind talking to younger boys. Short in stature, and rather untidy in appearance, he had the curious habit while walking of swinging his arms and legs until they seemed on the point of dropping off. It denoted an air of distraction that made him seem the same age as his brother, indeed even younger. Moreover, on that day, the company had the still rare privilege of being graced by the presence of its beloved teacher. And this, of course, was an inducement to discussion and controversy. Each of the students felt like a fighting cock, determined to outdo himself and get the better of his opponents.

"So tell me," the most belligerent one began, "if we do like Giorgio, don't we fall back into the Middle Ages?"

"Middle Ages?" Giorgio burst out. "Oh, come off it!"

"And that's not all. The Late Christian Middle Ages. All those genuflections, all that bigotry. Everything in that place is like a bad copy of a Catholic church."

"*Credo quia absurdum*," Giorgio's brother murmured seraphically. "But excuse me, I didn't mean to interrupt your discussion."

"Let's stick to the point," Giorgio insisted. "We don't worship images in that place, not even idols, which anyway is the same thing. All our worship is aimed at a book, and besides it's the Book par excellence, the highest document of moral law. As far as I'm concerned, it's of divine origin, but in any case. . ."

"In any case, no one understands what it's all about, and it's looked on with the same superstition that a Catholic has for a statue of Saint Anthony. Only your Catholic is more sincere. He doesn't commit sins of pride."

"The meaning of the Jewish religion," Giorgio retorted, "is the sanctification of every moment of existence. Every gesture, no matter how absurd or ridiculous, has a definite value. It's just a way of acknowledging ourselves to be children of the Covenant and part of the people of Israel."

"So isn't that racism, what you're saying?"

The speaker instinctively felt that he was on the side of reason. And he turned toward the teacher, hoping he would come to his aid with his oratorical skills. Was not rationality the very essence of his teaching? The rationality of history, not the abstract rationality of mathematicians. What was he waiting for? Why didn't he crush Giorgio with the weight of a single remark, the kind that hits the bull's eye, in a manner infinitely superior to faulty argumentation? The trouble was that the boys were not yet sufficiently aware of their teacher's taste for paradox, his constant urge to take the other side.

"Even if Giorgio is doing his best, as always, to make it seem the opposite, he's fundamentally right."

"What?"

"He offends people and doesn't succeed in convincing anyone. But I'll go so far as to say this: if I were to subscribe to a religion, I'd go back to that of the Jews."

"It's a religion like any other. It's superstition, it's intolerance. It's the persecution of Socrates and Spinoza."

"For one thing, religion, in the most profound and original sense of the word, means a bond, from the Latin *ligare*, to bind. It's one of the basic elements of man, a way of expressing his oldest social aspirations. When my father, who's an old-fashioned anticlerical, wants to make fun of the religion of his ancestors, he always says: 'Just think, according to the Jews, there have to be at least ten people just to say a prayer.' He's committing two errors of judgment, both of them naive. Because the fact of being ten in number means that the collectivity is more important than the individual, indeed that the individual is almost nothing when isolated from his social context. It's only a group, a people, a collectivity that can presume to raise itself to the level of God. And God, according to the Jewish tradition, is something very similar to the collectivity that worships him. Of course, the concepts aren't clear, and certain flashes of intuition are often hard to express. Sometimes a legend works better, like the one that says, if I remember correctly, that the *Shekhina*, which according to the mystics is the immanent majesty of God, went into exile along with the people of Israel."

Giorgio was beside himself with joy.

"And what would be your father's second error?"

"The word prayer. In the Bible, there are, to be sure, appeals for help or requests for protection. But most of the time they're poetic effusions. The Jewish synagogue chants, if rightly understood, are expressions of the people's joy and suffering—a great many of the psalms especially. Or else, they're stern declarations of collective laws, stamped in the memory of those who repeat them, according to the most effective of teaching methods, the one that Huxley prophesies for the brave new world of refined technology, but which in reality is very old, at least as old as the Bible. 'Hear, O Israel, the Lord our God, the Lord is one.' The Jews have been repeating it for centuries, and they've gone even further by literally applying the words of the Book: 'These commandments that I give thee shall be in thine heart: thou shalt bind them for a sign on thine hand, they shall be like frontlets between thine eyes, and thou shalt write them on the posts of thine house and on thy gates.' The Jews did it, and they still do it today, for this and the other essential commandments: thou shalt have no other gods but me, thou shalt not kill, thou shalt not steal, thou shalt not bear false witness. Looking further, we can see that the Bible doesn't limit itself to these moral precepts, but is minutely concerned with every gesture and moment of existence, how to wash, how to eat, how to avoid infectious diseases. These are prescriptions that also take on the character of a perpetual sanctification of man and the world: as you know, the rabbinical tradition has created blessings even for the most natural functions that we perform in private. At the root of all this is a brilliant intuition: only a sense of collective responsibility can guarantee man's salvation in this hostile world. And man's duty is to see, by his gestures and example, to the sanctification of the world."

"But those prescriptions are absurd. Like the prohibitions that go with observing the Sabbath."

"I wouldn't be so quick to dismiss them, if I were you. The Sabbath is a great and original discovery, which the heathen world hasn't yet understood. Think for a moment: for a whole day, an entire people, old and young alike, desists from its usual occupations, desists even from its work, even from the simplest preoccupations connected with the flesh—lighting a fire, cooking, carrying things—to concentrate on one single action."

"Prayer? . . . "

"We've already seen that that's not correct. It's study. The Temple, the 'sacred enclosure' of the Community's presidents, no longer exists among the Jews, and hasn't existed for a long time. It's the house of the collectivity, of the people, call it what you will. That's also what 'church,' in its original sense, means for the Christians, although they've forgotten it. It's the house where people study, where regularly every year, everyone rereads the Bible together from cover to cover—namely, the compendium of moral, juridical, and hygienic wisdom, as well as the poetic vocation of a people that has learned to use its mind. Do you realize what that means? If today all the peoples on earth were to devote one-seventh of their existence to the study of their nation's civic heritage, many problems wouldn't come up. In the Sabbath lies one of the great secrets of the survival of the Jewish people, which, let's not forget, has had no illiteracy for thousands of years, and is most certainly the sole survivor from those ancient times. And there also lies the explanation for its incorrigible pride and extraordinary intellectual arrogance."

"Quite uncalled-for, however, in the Jews of Rome. And probably a lot of other cities."

"The harsh living conditions in Rome, which continued without a break from the Counter-Reformation until the Italian state took over the city, explain a great many things. As does contact with papal culture, so different from that of the Jews."

"So, Professor, now you're putting in a good word for the popes!"

"Why not? It wouldn't be impossible. You have only to look at things from another standpoint. Instead of a religious and didactic system, to speak of a method of government. Between the empire and the papacy, I have no doubts as to which was the more effective and progressive, which institution embodied, for several centuries, the ideal of the many rather than the few, what today we call democracy. And systems, systems. . ."

"We already know you're a lover of paradoxes."

"No, read the history of the Church in the light of Machiavelli's ideas, which were very advanced for their time. And you'll be forced to modify many of your judgments."

"In any case, the concepts and habits of the Church don't exactly go with the tendencies you attribute to the Jews."

"Good God, can't you understand that everything in history is different, and that all of it can be explained just the same?"

"What about the genuflections before the scrolls of the Law? And the kisses, and all those other low superstitious gestures?"

Here Giorgio came to Monferini's defense.

"Yes, there's a lot of rubbish, and plenty of unconscious imitation of heathen rites. But we have to be careful on the subject of observances. Even the most absurd and insignificant act, if it's repeated often enough, can become an element of unity and brotherhood. It may be silly to say 'bless you' when someone sneezes, but people take it as a sign of benevolence and good manners. You can't expect the same intellectual commitment from everyone. That's why our rabbis say that the observance of a single precept counts for more than the study of the whole Law. But that's not all: the repetition of such gestures, which you can call mechanical and today it's partly true, has guaranteed our people's survival throughout the centuries."

Monferini was starting to make faces, and now it was hard to keep up the serious tone.

"But if the meaning of the content is lost, what's the point of surviving?"

"That's something we can't know," said Giorgio excitedly. "Along comes a Hitler and forces us, whether we like it or not, to look for the reason for our existence. And there it is, right in front of our eyes, handed down from generation to generation. All we have to do is interpret it. And that's what we've been doing for the past couple of hours."

The majority had been put on the defensive. The unexpected alliance between the traditional world and the modern secular one, represented by its most qualified exponent, had produced discomfiture and a great confusion of ideas.

"If that's the way you think, Professor, why don't you become a rabbi?"

The idea seemed so absurd, the image so far from any possibility of ever materializing, that everyone laughed—Giorgio, the stickler for tradition, first of all.

Monferini gave a little smirk, which was also a smile, since even in those years it was impossible for him to look serious.

"Crazy as it sounds, I could even be considered a rabbi: for centuries the Jews have been accustomed to turning things upside down in the most outlandish way. But I'd make a very bad rabbi, just as I'd make a very bad priest, because I'd reserve for myself complete freedom of thought—at least I think so. To be always on the side of what is just and true, and to be certain that truth is fluid and constantly changing—there's an abyss, I say, between these two positions. A rabbi or a priest possesses certain fragments of truth, often submerged in the trajectory of history. But he's tied to them forever, for him they become delights that he can't give up, even when they're shown to be false. I"—and here he lowered his voice to a subdued, almost confidential tone—"am a free man ready every day to pay a high price for my freedom. It's not even a merit, it's the way I was brought up, or, if you like, a form of self-intoxication. And I have no wish to impose my opinions on other people."

"Oh, no!" said Giorgio, in a burst of anger that also showed sincere admiration.

"Isn't this discussion the proof of it? And by the way, have you boys ever known a rabbi?"

It was a serious and undeniable failing. Here they had been talking in the abstract, and neglecting to go back to the source.

"So why not?" said Giorgio, a few days later. "Why don't we go and see the rabbi? You all know what the word means: our master, the one we recognize as being better educated than others. A rabbi isn't a priest, as you must know. And anyway we're old enough to defend ourselves."

Such sensible words, intended to strengthen resolve and instill courage, had just the opposite effect of rekindling shyness and muddling ideas still further.

"He's one of the leading authorities in the field of Jewish

studies, but on an international scale. I wouldn't think it makes him all that happy to be the head of a community like the one in Rome. But he'll certainly be glad to meet anyone who might someday become his pupil."

Besides being presumptuous and naive, Giorgio was very stubborn. He persisted and got the rabbi to give him an appointment at his home. But, so as not to complicate matters, he neglected to specify that he would not be coming alone.

It may have been just this deliberate but innocent omission that had a decisive effect on this important interview. Beyond his stony, sphinxlike appearance, the rabbi looked immediately perturbed by so tumultuous a group, which to him smelled of a plot, a joke, or, more seriously, something that might be seen as a political conspiracy. He listened with suspicious ears and eyes to the confused babble that the boys poured out, almost in chorus, and kept glancing anxiously at the door, as though an agent of the OVRA, the secret police, were lying there in wait. True, it was almost impossible to discern a logical thread in the tangle of concepts and overlapping propositions. But terms like Judaism and Jews, and names like Marx and Machiavelli, Freud and Jesus, recurred throughout, resounding like so many firecrackers at a country fair: they made noise and drew attention. When finally the boys remembered that they had come more to listen than to expound, there was a still more embarrassing moment.

The rabbi, originally from Galicia, had lived for a long time in Trieste, and spoke Italian haltingly. He looked at them for a long time, in cautious silence, uncertain about the best way to extricate himself.

"Good boys!" he said at last. "It's a huge consolation to see young people so eager to learn. Study is the noblest occupation, if it's pursued seriously, to the point of concentrating on it wholeheartedly and shunning the unessential. Life is what it is, but a scholar has many means for shunning the evil and frivolity of the world."

The rabbi, whose name had been Israel in his native village, now called himself Italo, to emphasize his complete identification with the fortunate Italian nation. Later, toward the end of his life, he was to convert to Christianity and call himself Eugenio, in honor of the reigning pope.

"Of course," he went on, "studying the Bible requires thorough preparation."

"We don't have much of that," Giorgio admitted. "But we do have a very great wish to study and don't want to wait. We'd like to begin examining the great problems of Judaism as soon as possible."

"But of course," said the rabbi, taken aback by Giorgio's impetuousness. "The important thing is to begin. I ask nothing better."

His expression hardened; his tone of voice became still more detached and professional.

"The first word of the Bible is *bereshit*, which means 'first of all,' 'in the beginning.' But there are a great many other meanings, which you aren't yet capable of understanding. There are thousands of important books on this subject. Let's take something easier, and closer to home: Adam, the first man. Adam is a name connected with the soil, *adama*. But what soil? Not just any soil, but a particular kind of red soil. *Adom* means red in Hebrew. An ancient Babylonian root. . ."

Once outside, no one had the heart to take it out on Giorgio. On the contrary, there was a great wish to cheer him up.

"After all, what's a rabbi?—just a man. He hasn't been ordained like a priest."

"And Jews aren't obliged to respect a hierarchy."

"All it takes is ten of them to form a community."

"So aren't there ten of us? Even more."

"And to get together any room will do."

"We're already in the habit of studying and discussing. Nobody can stop us from doing it on Friday night."

"So? Are you ready?"

"Of course. If you don't practice a religion, one day is as good as another."

"And would you be willing on that evening not to smoke?"

"Oh, no. It would be against our principles."

"But if the rest of you are smoking, I won't be able to resist."

A compromise was found. During the discussion no one would smoke, because, as the nonsmokers observed, it would make the air in the room unbreathable. Outside, each could do as he liked.

The following Friday, there were enough of them for a *minyan*, in accordance with tradition. Giorgio sported a magnificently embroidered *yarmulke*. Others covered their heads as best they could with folded handkerchiefs. But who cared about formalities? The only regret was the absence of Monferini. It might take a little patience, but sooner or later even he would show up: they were all convinced that he couldn't do without them.

Giorgio had the good sense to reduce the ceremonial part to a minimum. But he took the trouble to explain, as best he could, the meaning of words and gestures.

Baby-faced Giovannino, with his angelic features and shy movements—he never took part in the discussions and resented being called by the diminutive—lifted his voice, at first quaveringly, then gradually with more confidence, in the notes of "Lekhah Dodi," the trembling and impassioned song of an early sixteenth-century mystic:

> Come, my friend, to meet the bride,
> Sabbath, Sabbath, Sabbath Queen!

Then came the traditional word of blessing for the good things that man has found at his disposal: the fruits of the earth, bread, and wine. Concluding with the invocation, all the more touching because of the sad times: "May He who gives peace in heaven, give peace also to us and to all the people of Israel. Amen."

Being shut up in one room, they had no idea whether nightfall and the Sabbath had actually arrived. But all of them had entered into the Sabbath by a harmonious act of will, toppling a high barrier with no apparent effort.

The discussion, lively as always, went on until a fairly late hour. Their eyes shone, as with a superhuman intoxication. To come back down to earth, it would take many pairs of glasses, like the ones needed by Rabbi Zusya, the gentle fool of God, to distinguish the individual things of the world; otherwise, carried away by the rapture and fervor of his vision of the One God, he was unwittingly driven to see even the strangest and most diverse things as all one.

## V / THE TRUE MASTER OF THE NAME

In those days it was easy to stretch the Sabbath over the whole week. There was plenty of time, and the opportunities were endless. Rome, lazy and skeptical as ever, was under the illusion that it could weather the storm by ignoring it. Along with a few tolerable inconveniences, the war had brought several conspicuous advantages. There was no more automobile traffic. The streets had marvelous discoveries in store for anyone with eyes to see. To go on foot allowed you to discover their most mysterious and exciting secrets, which casual tourists would never know. It offered the almost irresistible opportunity to prolong the Sabbath of intellectual pleasures to its utmost limits. From the standpoint of the dogmatists, it must have been a great sin: it's scarcely conceivable, I won't say to a religious mind, but to an ordinary moralist, that a spiritual feast could go on forever. But meanwhile this is just what was happening. The students raised an infinite number of problems for themselves, but not that one.

Under Monferini's guidance, it was a season of great discoveries. Dostoevsky opened boundless horizons, revealing the voluptuousness of sin, and the tormenting pleasure of recognizing a collective guilt. The Karamazov brothers were companions for many months, and the gentle Alyosha, invisible but very much present, joined them on many journeys. And these torments did not contradict the deep conviction that very soon they would arrive at a systematic definition of man and the universe. Indeed, they acquired a constant certainty of it.

With Benedict Spinoza, the whole world seemed the purest geometry, the formulation and consequence of an original, brilliant proposition. But Giambattista Vico immediately provided another passkey to the cosmos, the alternation, in the historical process, of force and reason. With Kant, one arrived at a stated certainty that the apparent moving force of life, from our exclusive standpoint, is the intellect of man; and one recognized in this individuation the power as well as the limits of our minds, condemned for eternity to being essentially unknowable. But then immediately, with Hegel, one fell back into the old sin of total explanation of the metaphysical kind; the new driving force was the Ego, something very similar (by adding an "e" and dropping the "d") to the God of the ancients. The identification of the rational with the real re-echoed almost as obsessively as a popular song, and at certain times, and in the presence of certain people, even more. And already waiting in the wings were Marx and Freud and Bergson, each of whom held in his hand another lock-picking tool, different from the previous ones and for that very reason, it was hoped, more suited to the purpose. As for Judaism, it was something so elastic that it could adapt itself marvelously to any kind of conception: Hegelian or Marxist, atheist or psychological, as the case or wish might be.

In discussions on the street, at home, or at school there were no obstacles to the pursuit of these problems. But there was that business of the tram, which set limits. The tram still took up a considerable portion of the day, and it would have been ridiculous to waste it, but by its nature it lent itself better to whispering sweet nothings between lovers. In the heat of an argument, you couldn't help raising your voice. And words kept cropping up—such as progress and social revolution—that could spell trouble. The students had recourse to an invented vocabulary, in which Devonianism meant Marxism and palingenesis the workers' revolution. But what couldn't be avoided, from time to time, were the protests of errand boys and tram conductors, already poorly paid for the work they had to do and by no means disposed to make it more oppressive by listening to such lectures. Their remonstrances brought a keen sense of pain, since they were voiced by qualified members of the working class. But it was reassuring to think that it could only have been the dictatorship that had squelched the tram workers' taste for controversial subjects. No one doubted that with time they would once more learn to drive their vehicles while arguing about the theory of surplus value, so important for their spiritual salvation.

Music was another point of contact. Those who not long ago had warbled "Maria La-O," or even sillier tunes like the one about the hapless nitwit Pippo, would now just as soon have forgotten all about it. Concerts and record collections were revealing the treasures of the Romantic heritage, the tempests of Beethoven, the torments of Brahms, and the sorrowing preciosities of a Chopin or a Rachmaninov. This then was an adventure that made the students particularly proud, because of the absence of Monferini, ordinarily their spiritual guide. Disoriented and tone-deaf when it came to music, he had to stay out of it, and for the boys this was a proof of self-emancipation, despite their continuing fondness for him. Giorgio, too, the other dominating influence in the group, held an isolated position. By a typical taste for contradiction, his preferences went to the two extremes on the horizon, Mozart and Stravinsky, though the combination is certainly less fortuitous than it seems. But in the middle he placed Verdi's operas, which were indeed a conspicuous feature of his way of life. The interweaving of farce, superstition, and tragedy in the quintet and *concertato* of *Un Ballo in maschera* rightly seemed to him one of the high points of the human comedy; and the beautiful, vigorous love duet in the third act, with the arrival of Renato and the sudden entrance of the conspirators, under that disconcerting "*raggio lunar del miele*," was for him marvelously resolved in the final mocking allusion to the frantic gossip in the city. But this was not all. Giorgio, much as he loved Verdi, had an equal and passionate love for his librettists. If you asked him about the prospects of his tragic love affairs, he would reply by shaking his head: "*Un dì, quando le veneri il tempo avrà fugate . . .*" Of a successful rival, he said: "*l'amante e amato giovine.*" When, much later, in truly tragic circumstances, he was asked to explain why he had given up his youthful passions in order to concentrate all his love on the woman who is still his life companion, the only words he could find were these: "She loved me for my misfortunes, and I loved her for her compassion." Considering the circumstances, it was a justifiable way to put it. But no one could ever forgive him the time he confirmed an appointment by announcing: "*Ivi saranno i miei.*" He thus made everyone wear his best clothes, with neckties and other bourgeois accouterments, in the expectation that his parents, the engineer Augusto and the very proper Signora Virginia, were coming too. They didn't, of course, but who would have expected Giorgio to adopt for the occasion, by an inscrutable association of ideas, the words spoken by the gloomy Amonasro when he learns the secret of the Napata gorges from Radames's careless lips? Moreover, he uttered them with the same stammering diction as the baritone amid the uproar of the kettledrum and brasses on the stage.

There wasn't much to see at the movies, Fascism having banned almost all foreign films. But there was a place on the Via Borgognona (torn down some years ago to make way for a supermarket) where retrospective screenings were held in the afternoon, and if you could put up with the poor quality of the reels, you were able to enjoy the masterpieces of the history of cinema: the German expressionists, the Soviet masters, and especially the cheerful eccentricities of René Clair. French films were among the few authorized to cross the threshold of cultural clubs. The craze for *le film noir*, with the ever equivocal and decadent Jean Gabin as hero, allowed Fascism to point out to Italian audiences the depravity and sadness with which the traditional democracies were tinged: you see, the French aren't having children; this is the result of lost potency and too much free time. Thus a Jean Gabin could easily pass from the suicide of *Le jour se lève* to the foul depravity of *La bête humaine*, clear proof of how the working class could be corrupted by bad customs and the worst sort of companions. And Jules Berry, with his face of a good fellow gone rotten, personified the other side of the coin, a bourgeoisie corrupted by its own prosperity and its inveterate habit of deserting the nuptial bed.

In exploring the paths of cinema, the guide was Roberto, who even managed to found Orsa Film, a microscopic production house that never succeeded in completing its first film. Not for any lack of ideas, but a lack of resources. But no one drew from this any deductions about the solid connections always needed in the real cinema world between talent and business. Everyone at the time was convinced that ideas were enough.

Also there was always the Fascist youth organization Cineguf: it cost almost nothing and they didn't bother to ask students for a racial ID card. Here the more common types of films prevailed, light comedies of the kind known as "white telephones," alternating with colossal epics extolling the Fascist regime. If you tried hard enough, you could imagine you saw—and probably they were there—the first efforts to swim against the tide, impulses, vague as they were, against conformism and rhetoric. Little as it was, it already seemed like a lot. Moreover, Sunday morning at Cineguf was always the prelude to a traditional stroll along the Via Veneto, still humanly acceptable in its bourgeois indolence.

But among all forms of entertainment, the theater was the cheapest. In wartime, when the blackout made evening performances virtually impossible as the occasion for society parties and a setting for gossip, the theater once again acquired a chaste pride, and reassumed a character of pure and austere nobility. It became an encounter, on sad holiday afternoons, between a few pathetic actors, left stranded for lack of other resources, and a handful of spectators, most of them students. Every material interest had been laid aside. The actors were struggling chiefly to survive and maintain their self-esteem, and as for the students, almost all of them were hangers-on of Riccardo the cripple, who for years had been organizing the claque for the principal theaters in Rome. Under these conditions, and perhaps only under them, could the theater go back to being something that had to do with culture.

Riccardo hung out in the Galleria San Marcello, the strategic point of access for the best orchestra seats, or boxes, to be more precise. There was always a small crowd waiting for him, boys who showed considerable nervousness, since no one had ever been able to figure out his criteria for giving away tickets. To have known if he looked at the appearance of one's clothes, or limited himself to weighing, from some secret vantage point, the intensity of the applause, would have provided a clue. But Riccardo arrived in perfect silence, despite his game leg, and still in silence handed out the pink, green, and blue tickets that he had in his hand. He stared into the eyes of each of the boys who stood before him, and in the depths of his mind made the irrevocable decision, either handing him the ticket or, unforeseeably, passing him by.

The winners felt boundless pride, the rejected an incomprehensible humiliation.

Thanks to Riccardo, and to Anton Giulio Bragaglia, who carried his impudent couldn't-care-less attitude to the point of passing himself off as an Irish nationalist, one was able to sample the complicated concoctions of the American playwright Eugene O'Neill, then all the rage for their mixture of naturalism and Ibsenism, with a large dose of incest and Freudian guilt complexes. But it was their moment, and the moment was long enough to strain the limits of human endurance. To see *Strange Interlude* and *Mourning Becomes Electra* put the strength of one's spirit to the test, almost as much as Wagner's *Ring* cycle, but with fruits of more dubious flavor.

Sometimes the lucky acquisition of a box seat allowed one to witness the unbounded perfidy of great actors. One evening, it was almost immediately obvious that Emma Gramatica, famous for her d'Annunzio roles and now incredibly old (and yet she would live another twenty-five years), was unable to stomach the presence of a young beginner, playing the part of a servant girl, and who in addition to being young was also very pretty. Every now and then Gramatica could be heard to mutter: "Who put her in my play? She's a bitch . . ." Until they came to the crucial scene in the second act, when the girl stepped forward and began speaking the one important line that the script allowed her: "Madam, madam, something horrible has happened . . ." But the sweet old lady interrupted her with an imperious gesture, and delighting the audience as always, ad-libbed: "I know all about it, my girl. My husband has strangled his young mistress, and now he's killed himself. They're lying there in a huge pool of blood. The shadow of tragedy hangs over this unfortunate family. Just go away, my dear, and leave me to my sorrow."

Ruggero Ruggeri's offerings were more substantial. In the

beautiful setting of the Teatro Argentina his highly musical voice, scarcely audible, rose to capture the attention of the small audience and guide it toward an appreciation of Pirandello. These were not his dramas of the dreary Italian provinces, for which the students would have been largely unprepared. Rather it was the subtle disintegration of noble souls, disgusted by the various forms of madness that the world calls logic, or decorum, or common sense, or social convention. And these heroes of emotional awareness— Henry IV, Baldovino, Martino Lori—fought always with the same weapons of human madness—logic, convention, common sense—but with unfailing consequences all the way to the end. They accepted the hypocrisy of others at its face value, and even made it their shield, impregnable on all sides. But inevitably they fell victim to their own rigor, trapped in a a bitter solitude, for which—as for the world crumbling around them—they saw no glimmer of a solution.

These performances did nothing to conceal the extreme poverty caused by the war. The swaying curtain of painted canvas, the shabbiness surrounding the leading actor, even his modest bourgeois air, now quite remote from the splendors of the d'Annunzian period, oddly enough came together to re-create the more genuine Pirandello, who rightly appeared to these youngsters as the most merciless diagnostician of the prevailing sickness and its true origins. Perhaps one day even the most obstinate Fascists, removing their melodramatic black shirts, would examine themselves like Pirandello's characters. And would repeat in a quite different tone, as happened to Ruggeri himself, the words of the once so violent and bloody Aligi: "Mother, mother, I slept for seven hundred years; seven hundred years, and I come from far away . . ."

This passion for the footlights led the students to go searching about for other places, close enough at hand, or at least within the city limits. I mean those now almost extinct forms of variety theater that were known as curtain-raisers: a series of more or less new songs, sung by someone who, like Pasquariello or Gabrè, may have seen better days; the suggestive appearance of Alfredo Bambi in his *Fattaccio* (Crime Story); the pitiful high kicking of the "Seven Stars, Seven," who might better have been called, in view of the food shortages of the time, "Seven Starving Young Ladies—And Then There Were Six." But these were interesting outings, sometimes. In the austere climate brought on by the war, they made it possible to rediscover, with a little luck and a good deal of imagination, a comic spirit different from the bloated one of the Italian bourgeois tradition: a rather desolate and funambulist comic spirit, composed of absurd gestures, a show of timidity, and a few inconclusive words. At the Brancaccio or the Principe, or in some other outlying theater, there was a new comedian who entertained the audience by joking about his diminutive stature, and creating over it the parody of a very tall cuirassier. Unfortunately for us and his career, he soon became a success, developed a paunch, and lost his original vein of inspiration. But three contortionist brothers, who stuttered slogans, not only absurd but incomprehensible, from which only the single word *polenta!* (corn meal) emerged, appealed to a genuine and long-lasting familiarity with poverty and captured the audience's imagination more. Two of them eventually faded away into silence and absolute poverty, but the third still appears from time to time in some film or television comedy: he has kept the features of a spoiled brat and signifies the congenital ability to be a bore and a nuisance. He has a particular and inimitable way of walking, which serves to distract attention from the thinness of his material.

This kind of comic talent is less instinctive than it looks. Very often it is the product of art: it takes the mechanical gesture and its result and subjects them to long, often centuries-old practice, whereby the device has been perfected over several generations through the meticulous and imperceptible improvement of turns and pratfalls. Its roots are almost always sunk in an unconsciously rich soil of social and cultural protest. It has its most convincing and most vivid example in Charlie Chaplin, the greatest mime of modern times, he too a product of art, born in the slums of the most crowded metropolis of nineteenth-century Europe—a true genius when it comes to stagecraft and calculated effects, and a cool manipulator of other people's emotions, in a calibrated alternation between laughter and tears. Charlie Chaplin, though no one has ever been certain of it, is said to have been of Jewish extraction, as some of his facial features would suggest, as well as his surname, possibly a corruption of Kaplan, behind which may lurk an original Cohen—as happens with a lot of Italian priests.

Chaplin was a thorny subject in those days. His films were no longer shown, except for a few reels surviving here and there in some private collection. Fascism had completely ostracized a man who stood at the antipodes of its heroic and totalitarian concepts. Its aversion for the trembling little anarchist was as instinctive as it was absolute and ruthless. But no regime, no matter how vigilant, can close the sluice gates to the countless rivulets into which the great river of history— which is, whether we like it or not, the river of culture as well—is dispersed and flows.

Satire of the modern world and its relentless incongruities could also be forbidden; and naturally in wartime, one didn't even speak about parodying the dictatorship. But it might happen that in some attic or secluded cubbyhole, one would come across an old dog-eared, dust-covered book, and that from its pages, as though by magic, strange little personages would step forth, whimsical in their darkly angelic expressions, perpetually moving in a frantic dance, of which it was impossible to say whether it meant convulsions, mimetic parody, or mystical rapture. This is more or less how the students' encounter with the Hasidim, those touching figures of Eastern Europe, took place.

Martin Buber had evoked them with feeling and a concern that was perhaps too scholarly. His reconstruction of the Hasidic world is filtered through several lenses of contemporary Western culture. Other testimonies, such as Langer's, are more direct and true to life; in them one breathes not only the poverty that creates populism and folklore, but the actual smell of small Eastern Jewish villages. But Buber's book was the only document available to Monferini's students.

The poetic figure of the holy Baal Shem, the exponent of dancing as an instrument of redemption and elevation, he who in the synagogue crowded with praying men awaited the shrill whistle of a little boy to declare that God's wrath was over, and preached "love yourselves more, be more at ease"—this absurd precept impressed itself deeply on these adolescent minds sharpened by their familiarity with Kant. It seemed, and was, the revelation of a more human world, in which knowledge, power, and wealth appeared as instruments of senseless oppression. The absurd became the holy and healing need of man, considered merely as a part of the whole, albeit an essential one: "If a man sings and cannot raise his voice, and another comes to his aid, then the first one also succeeds in raising his voice." And from this leveling there sprang, unexpectedly, a re-evaluation of man himself, whom Jewish mystics have called the companion of the sixth day of Creation: "a ladder planted on the earth, and whose summit reaches the heavens: all his gestures, acts, and words leave traces on the higher world."

The Baal Shem's disciples obeyed their master's exhortations; they scattered all over the world and carried his message with them. Even today in the America of Ford and Rockefeller you may run into a young ascetic—red-haired like Jesus the Nazarene—wrapped in a black silk caftan, his regal head covered with a foxskin cap: he is a descendent of Israel ben Eliezer, nicknamed the Baal Shem Tov, the True Master of the Name. Even in modern Jerusalem, with its trade unions and utilitarian outlook, it is easy to encounter such figures. And in London and Cape Town as well. Chagall's paintings, if nothing else, have transplanted their features to every part of the civilized world. But sometimes the various Zusyas, Davids, and Elkonens have assumed unexpected disguises, difficult to recognize, either out of necessity or instinct, or simply out of the old Jewish taste for simulation.

Rabbi Baruch's grandson was once playing hide-and-seek with another boy. He hid and waited a long time, thinking that the boy was looking for him and unable to find him. But at last he emerged from his hiding place, and not seeing his friend, realized that he hadn't even looked for him. He ran to his grandfather's room, crying and accusing his false playmate. With tears in his eyes, Rabbi Baruch said: "God says the same thing."

One need only reverse this allegorical anecdote—it is man who seeks God and doesn't find him, either because he's not there or doesn't want to show himself—to arrive at the poetics of Franz Kafka, the greatest interpreter of modern insecurity, and find the key to his mysterious novels, *The Trial* and *The Castle*.

While the discovery of the Hasidim was fortuitous, that of Kafka was one of many due to Monferini. Often he would toss a book with a strange title in front of his students, muttering, "Take a look at this stuff, if you can manage to digest it." This was how he had presented Melville's *Moby-Dick*, recently translated by Cesare Pavese, who was an old friend of Monferini's and living in Rome at the time. But he stayed holed

up, gruff as a bear, discontented with himself and the world—
today we can see he had reasons—in an apartment on the Via
Savoia, the temporary offices in Rome of the publisher Ein-
audi.

"The Metamorphosis" and *The Castle* quickly sparked debate, as was to be expected, since Kafka lent himself—and
still does—to every sort of interpretation. The psychologist
and the physician, the socialist and the bourgeois, the atheist
and the believer, the simple man and the intellectual, are
able to encounter themselves and their most secret problems
in him. The world as they perceive it in dreams or moments
of total isolation. As well as the exact opposite. What one
desires and what one fears form the substance of Kafka's
plots. Much as he may be modeled after his tormented creator, the hero, in his lack of determination, mirrors an enormous number of human beings—men, a great many men, so
as not to abuse the binding word humanity, but which comes
naturally in the presence of a genuine work of art.

Furthermore, Kafka was a Jew, and his Judaism, to those
fresh from the experience of Hasidism, was beyond question.
Certain characters, like the messengers from the gloomy castle, seemed lifted bodily, barely buoyed by the writer's subdued and discreet voice, from the little fables of the Eastern
rabbis. And the nature of their contents apart (but does not
*The Trial* have a splendid precursor in the biblical Book of
Job? Is not the problem of the inscrutability and of the very
existence of divine justice the same?), even more surprising
affinities were revealed. The brief parables of Franz Kafka had
the same precise pace, the same essential concentration, and
even the same moral foundation as the exemplary little tales
dear to the Hasidic tradition: genuine bravura pieces where,
in the same way as in a well-devised gag, every word, every
gesture, and even every pause lead inevitably to the punch-
line. In "The Bridge" this exercise of skill is all too obvious,

while in the parable "The Next Village," the moral cannot be separated from the technique.

In those wartime days, there was no way of verifying any conjectures about Kafka's involvement in Jewish life, other than the mere fact of his birth. One would have to wait for the postwar period, when culture began to circulate once more, to discover evidence of his interest in the Yiddish theater, amply documented in his diaries, and still more, his meeting with Buber in Berlin, and with other investigators of Jewish customs in all their most mysterious manifestations.

Meanwhile the students debated as always, and made guesses. Not, however, without heated arguments. Monferini restated his opinion about the essential as well as desperate irony of a writer who has arrived at the understanding that beyond man lies the void. In support of his conviction, he had no qualms about tampering with the most beautiful and poetic passages. The girls were repelled by the transformation of human beings into insects. They swore they didn't believe it themselves, and that they were only horrified at the thought that someone more vulnerable might take it seriously.

Giorgio, the stickler for tradition, revealed his true nature as a relentless secularist, rationalist, and organizer of exuberantly divine confusion. Not for nothing did he adore the music of Mozart, in which bursting genius is always channeled into fluid, crystalline harmony. Kafka's tormented symbolism had nothing to say to him. The very name sounded to his ears (this is a little embarrassing to mention, but after all it's history) like an odd, disagreeable combination of *caca* and *café*. With all the respect he felt for the age-old sufferings of the Diaspora, he dreamed of something quite different for the Jewish people.

## VI / PRAISE AND CELESTINE

One day a boy, neither too bright nor too backward, went to confide in Monferini, his valiant teacher and friend. Exams were coming up, and he was almost sure he would manage to scrape through, except for the holy terror he felt at the prospect of the science orals. For all his intelligence and will power, he very much doubted that he would be able to overcome the obstacle represented by Donna Maria's questions. "Try to get her to feel sorry for you," suggested Monferini, with his rather too easy optimism. That's all very well, but how do you get tears out of an inorganic substance? "I don't know about a stone," remarked Monferini, his mind already on something else, "but a woman is always a woman—just find some moving story to tell her."

The boy pondered this advice and came up with a story so complicated that it would be a pity if it were lost, especially these days when there's a dearth of good sentimental stories. He let on to Donna Maria that, for all his heightened intellectual efforts, he was unable to keep his mind on anything, whether it be science or any other subject. He had got involved with a girl who was threatening to kill herself if he didn't marry her. It would be a pleasure to marry her, as well as a good deed, but how could he get out of his family's insistence that he marry a rich heiress, whom they'd already picked out for him, and who moreover was physically unattractive because she was suffering from the after-effects of a serious illness? The heiress took drugs to dull her pain, as did the would-be suicide, to resist the temptation to throw herself from the parapet by the river; and he, being unable to buy drugs because he was a minor, was thinking of going abroad and enlisting in the Foreign Legion—assuming it still existed. The result of this whole story was that the exam was limited to a single question, the formula for water. Donna Maria distractedly supplied the answer herself: "$H_2O$."

Prior to the other exams, there was a series of early-morning private interviews, held in the chemistry lab. One by one the pupils in the class filed in, and by the flickering light of the Bunsen burner some alarming situations were revealed. Almost all the boys confessed to being involved in drug trafficking, or at the very least of having taken too many sleeping pills. Many of the girls complained of troublesome glandular problems. Stories of potential incest and Oedipus complexes came out, and gloomy tales of love so unhappy it would have taken the hand of God to resolve them. It was the first year in the memory of man that none of Donna Maria's pupils had to suffer the indignity of make-up exams in the fall.

Unfortunately, it was also the last. At the supper organized to celebrate the students' promotions, someone, his mind clouded with wine, insisted on making jokes and claiming to be able to reveal the truth of the whole matter. He committed an even more serious imprudence by attributing its origin and paternity to Monferini, who had done nothing except to suggest telling a moving story. But Donna Maria was not amused, and the supper did not end on the same happy note with which it began.

This little episode has been recalled to throw light on certain things that happened in the Jewish School and the atmosphere that prevailed there during the years of the Second World War.

Monferini had gradually introduced, one step at a time, a veritable revolution into the school. The students had welcomed it enthusiastically, and Donna Maria, isolated in the chemistry lab, had seen the day-by-day diminution of the specter of her terrifying quizzes, hovering like a sinister shadow between the Lungotevere Sanzio and the Piazza del Collegio Romano, that is to say, between the Jewish School and the famous Liceo Visconti, where she had taught before. But even Torquemada's Inquisition, with the passage of time, has been transformed into an anxious memory, then into a bogey for immature minds, until it has reached its present dimensions: a proverbial way of speaking, a subject for erudite pedants, and from time to time, alas, the subject of jokes.

Monferini's destructive campaign had attacked from the start one of the most potent weapons of Donna Maria and the traditional school system: namely, marks, that verdict that scars a person's life. The complicated alchemy of a 5-plus or a 6-minus-minus, or the threat of an irrevocable 3, had been dissolving like the anathema of the Church fathers before the impetuous gusts of the winds of reason. It has been a long time since *Anathema sit* has scared anyone. The day will come, stated Monferini's enlightened creed, when it will be the same for a 4 in philosophy, which unfortunately even today appears to legions of students as the most disgraceful condemnation, like *vitando*, the more serious degree of excommunication.

He had started at the top by belittling the value of the highest marks. If someone to whom he had assigned, after a test, the average, highly acceptable mark of 6 complained, Monferini proved to be entirely sympathetic. "Not good enough? Too low for you? Don't worry, I can give you a 7, an 8, even a 9, whatever you like." And he made as though to enter it in the record. "Since marks are so important in life. If tomorrow you get in trouble with the Germans, you can always tell them: I got an 8 in history and philosophy." But already the student was asking him to do what he thought best, the 6 would be fine, he didn't care about getting a higher mark... The main thing was to put an end to this discussion, which the rest of the class found much too entertaining, as did Monferini himself, of course, despite the sly and hypocritically affable expression he assumed for the occasion.

In more embarrassing cases, those of disastrous failure involving consistently poor performance, Monferini disclaimed responsibility: "You've put me in a real fix. So now give yourself a mark. Let's see what you think you deserve." The verdict was almost always too harsh, and it was then up to him to restore the balance, not for the thing in itself, of course, but so as not to exclude the possibility of a last-minute reprieve.

In the end, the whole question of marks was the subject of a closed debate, where they were criticized and radically demolished. They could not, however, be eliminated. Down in the chemistry lab, Donna Maria was upholding them like a banner and a matter of honor: now she was claiming the right to keep a student's success or failure strictly secret so that he would have more time to ponder his uncertain future. Furthermore, there were the final exams at the end of the year, which would be held before a government commission. But Monferini shook his head, and along with his head his hair: he would have nothing to do with this stupid reckoning; what counts, he said, is the overall evaluation, the teacher's belief and the student's as well. Or rather, marks would be acceptable if they were reciprocal, if the pupil could also assign them to the teacher, and they then took the average—a plan that could not, however, be carried out since it undermined the very idea of authority. And besides, frankly, who would feel like giving a mark to Donna Maria? He, however, had no

intention of giving any: this was a freedom he was not relin-
quishing, one of the few granted him by the regime.

A compromise solution was adopted. He would wash his
hands of the whole business, and the notorious marks would
be the result of collective deliberation. In other words, the
class would decide. But without any fuss, without quibbling
and wasting time. Because marks, good or bad, were not all
that important in life.

This little reef having been circumnavigated—but it's the
reefs that lie just below the surface of the water that sink
ships—another battle began, aimed at the very figure of the
"teacher." What is a teacher? A poor graduate, more or less
trained, who is condemned to stir the same watery soup for
the rest of his life. His only hope is to have sufficiently bright
students. Otherwise it means boredom and anxious yawns
for the whole class, and slow death for the teacher.

There was no reason why the class shouldn't take his place
as much as possible. If the students were mature enough,
they could very well prepare themselves by researching a
certain number of lessons. The discussion would then be
open, and with the democratic consent of the class, the
teacher too would take part. It was an insidious trap that
forced the top students, spurred on by unspeakable pride, to
carry out exhausting research on the subject assigned. To the
point—and it was a just revenge—where they sometimes
embarrassed even him. What was he supposed to know about
some of Kant's youthful escapades or the gastronomical tastes
of Schopenhauer? And how was he to know the spiritual
itinerary of someone like Salomon Maimon, protégé of Moses
Mendelssohn and a wanderer through half of Europe? In the
end, however, it turned out that this Maimon, much as he was
ignored in current literature, was a figure of some importance: Kant himself had appreciated his talent, and some of
his writings, but especially his vagabond life truly deserved

attention. Meanwhile several students had been allowed to occupy the teacher's chair and conduct classes, enough for Monferini's cynical manipulation. Busy as always at his job as assistant principal, he immediately raised them on his own authority to the rank of substitute teachers and turned them loose on various classes whenever the actual teacher was absent.

This was a slippery slope, which led the brightest, and most naive, straight to the weekly meetings of the ADEI, the Italian Association of Jewish Women.

Racial persecution, and then the war, had swept away what had been rather pompously called the cultural life of Italian Jewry. And yet, in the years between the two great wars, its fragile structure had been shaken by ferments that were by no means negligible. Perhaps not in Rome, where the Jews still seemed benumbed by the age-old presence of the temporal; nor in Turin, where the Risorgimento had almost abolished distinctions among citizens of different religions; but in other parts of Italy there had been some movement. In Trieste, the traditional Hapsburg tolerance had helped to produce a heightened intellectual climate, and for several years the position of rabbi there had been filled by a sharp-witted young man, short in stature, who also edited a small and lively newspaper. Dante Lattes had sprung from the fertile soil of Tuscany, where the streams of two great cultures, the Jewish and the Italian, had long learned to coexist. Lattes, who bore in his name the bright omen of the father of the Italian tongue, and who until his final days was engaged in translating Manzoni's *I promessi sposi* into modern Hebrew, followed the teachings and tradition of the two leading Italian Jewish masters of the nineteenth century: the mystic Elia Benamozegh and the rationalist Shemuel David Luzzatto. It was especially in Leghorn that worthy rabbis and educators had emerged from Benamozegh's line. In Florence, a group of young men of various backgrounds and intelligence, but all possessed of lively enthusiasm, had assembled around another master, Margulies, who was not, however, of Italian origin. Over them emerged the figure of a strange red-bearded apostle, the lawyer Alfonso Pacifici, an eloquent preacher and advocate of what was called "integral Judaism"; but so convinced a champion that, in his long and fortunately still thriving life, he has gradually detached himself from all organized groups within Judaism, and lives today in Jerusalem, separated even from the most intransigeant orthodox factions, and standing on his own in accordance with a tradition whose roots go back to Tuscany.

In 1924, a famous Youth Congress was held in Leghorn, attended by those mentioned above and two other young men, Enzo Sereni and Nello Rosselli. The differences among them seemed profound, and certainly it was impossible to reconcile the conflicting traditions—Italian and Jewish—as well as those trends for which the various speakers made themselves the spokesmen: the integral religion of Alfonso Pacifici, the historical enlightenment of Nello Rosselli, and the working-class Zionism of Enzo Sereni, who was one of the very few Roman participants. From Leghorn, however, a fresh breeze of renewal and a mixture of ideas spread across the scattered Jewish communities, arriving even in slumbering Rome. Newspapers were founded or consolidated, and cultural clubs proliferated.

All of this, as I said, was swept away by the war. At the time of the government-sponsored Jewish School, Sereni, Lattes, and Pacifici had, as was to be expected, found refuge in Palestine, while Nello Rosselli, along with his brother Carlo, had fallen victim to a Fascist ambush in France, a country that had welcomed a large number of Italian intellectuals. The movers and shakers of the Italian Jewish community having left the scene, while periodicals and cultural clubs were stifled by violence or deprivation, nothing survived but the ADEI, the Italian Association of Jewish Women. And this was the first training ground, outside the classroom, for the new generation.

Once a week ladies who were free of household duties, and who were still attracted by the tradition of heated discussion, met in a small auditorium on the Lungotevere Sanzio, not far from the building assigned to the Jewish School. Most of them were fairly well along in years, elder sisters who were still unmarried, aunts who had finally discarded the idea of marriage, nice little grandmothers, their white hair crowned by hats from the turn of the century, who by now had trained their husbands and children more or less to look after themselves. They knitted and embroidered, more out of the old habit of keeping their hands busy than for those charitable works that constituted one of the reasons for their organization. And while the yarn mounted on their needles, they had no objection to listening to a speaker.

But speakers were hard to find. Every year the rabbi spoke, on some abstruse element of Assyro-Babylonian semantics, and the ladies nodded their heads, hoping, but without much confidence, that he would think they were paying attention. Then the daughter of the same rabbi, a beautiful blond girl with modern tendencies, spoke on women's duties according to the biblical tradition, of which there are a great many, and their rights, which are almost nonexistent, inasmuch as the woman is considered almost a patrimonial possession of the man. But this, the girl explained, merely heightened the sublime mission of sacrifice incumbent on Jewish wives and mothers, following in the wake of the splendid tradition of Sarah, Rebecca, and Rachel. Again the listeners nodded their heads, being certainly convinced, while the speaker herself appeared somewhat less so. The exciting revelation, whose source could not be doubted, that the name Rachel, by its ancient root, means "ewe" aroused nervous giggles, since the first lady of Italy—or if not of Italy, let's say of the Romagna—was Donna Rachele Mussolini. All heads turned to look at the only man present, who was also always the first to take a seat in the hall, always the same seat in the back. But the cause of so much concern appeared to be deep in his detached thoughts, perhaps of the distant Sicily from which hunger had driven him, or of the nearby police station, where he and his colleagues vied for the easy assignment of supervising a lecture at the ADEI—thoughts so deep and restful that, lulled by the droning voice of the speaker, he had fallen into a sound sleep. But, after all, a policeman must be ready to catch a quick nap wherever he can, even if it's on a chair.

After the rabbi and his daughter, came the turn of a bearded young psychoanalyst, who although promising was still short of patients. His hobbyhorse, of course, was Freud, who, luckily for Jewish cultural clubs, was born and died a Jew. The controversies surrounding his life and career provided the opportunity for an endless exposition of psychiatric history, its principal tendencies, its conflicts with psychology, and its best known clinical cases expounded from European and American lecture platforms: a long list of names, famous and unknown, from academic biographies and clinical files, which increased the nodding movements of the ladies' heads, absolutely convinced as they were that it was still a question of Jewish names, distinguished for whatever the cause. Nor was this such a rash hypothesis, considering that Jews, sometimes for their own reasons, sometimes not, have always made an outstanding contribution to the list of mental disorders.

Meanwhile the policeman had sunk into an even deeper and more relaxed sleep. His showy black moustaches did not detract from the angelic look on his face—on the contrary, they enhanced it.

Following the psychoanalyst, the ladies of the ADEI had the problem of picking a speaker for their next meeting. The choice was very limited, less for the brilliance of the speakers than for their inability to speak on any other subject but the one they cared about, and which they had already abundantly treated. Each had his hobbyhorse, and it was always the same. Thus Giorgio's brother, the compliant engineer, knew only one subject, fascinating as it was, the Book of Job. And the conclusion that he unfailingly reached, as paradoxical as it was obvious in advance, was that Job, despite traditions, rationalist critics, and the Lord himself, was to be considered guilty.

A brilliant lawyer, in an overdocumented prosecutor's speech, demonstrated in no uncertain terms that Josephus, the apologist for the Flavian dynasty, was the most despicable traitor to the Jewish people. Whereupon, taking the side of the defense, and with an equal wealth of evidence and quotations, he demonstrated that Josephus was a kind of national hero, infinitely superior to poor Simon bar Ghiora, who not for nothing had ended his days in the Mamertine Prison. This, frankly, was too much even for the charming ladies of the ADEI, who did not care to be distracted from their knitting by such intense emotions.

The only person not disturbed by this cold shower was the excellent policeman, who aside from his deep sleep, was used to the ups and downs of courtrooms, the verbal acrobatics of lawyers, and the outbursts they produced.

Thus, by a kind of inevitability—the course of history, as we know, runs on the iron tracks of necessity—the ladies of the ADEI found themselves obliged to turn to Monferini's students, who, in their turn, had been unwittingly trained for this very purpose. The one who stayed out of this encounter, which might even have turned into a clash, was precisely that diabolical manipulator of souls, the secret instigator of so many crises and second thoughts; but to have brought Mon-ferini to the ADEI would really have been too blatant, like forcing a Marat or a Robespierre on a reception in honor of a Mother Superior and her nuns, or nowadays bringing one of the ecumenical fathers of Vatican II before the—fortunately dissolved—tribunal of the Holy Inquisition. Once again, the only one not to be shocked would have been the policeman asleep in his chair.

A devastating blast of wind blew into the hall where so much dust had accumulated over the years. Hats and veils flew off, coiffures were ruffled, knitting wool and embroidery thread got tangled. Among the new arrivals there was one who proclaimed himself God Almighty in person, without bothering, in his hurry, to explain the reasons that had suggested to him an identification between the stern God of our fathers and the Ego understood in its conceptual transfiguration. The tormented Franz Kafka with his problems, unresolvable in their very formulation, and his anxieties, a mingling of despair and satisfaction, became a regular guest, a familiar face to the aunts and grandmothers, who, in their turn, felt called upon to confide in him their own problems and anxieties: how to tell the head of the family that the household allowance was not enough to last to the end of the month, and what were the proper measures of ingredients for baking puff pastries and Passover cookies.

Giorgio, who was undoubtedly the one most cut out to impress the gathering, turned out, possibly due to exaggerated expectations, to be the most bitterly disappointing to the dear ladies. He was the living embodiment of the spirit of contradiction. He would dig up the least known episode, the most humble and seemingly insignificant character, and make everything in his talk hinge on them. Always, of course, he was concerned with the great themes of universal cosmogony and Jewish history—and Jewish history, it should be remembered, had already reached the year 5729. Not to mention that, sooner or later, you again found yourself confronting—and it was hard to see how it had happened—the delicate harmony of Mozart and the seeming din of early Stravinsky.

Very often this ideal hinge was Yochanan ben Zakkai, or John, son of Innocent, to give a correct but colorless translation of his name. With a little patience, it was possible to discern in the vicissitudes of his life several keys whereby to investigate the Jewish past and its painful present. Already the episode connected with his name, the innocence of someone presumed to be guilty, demonstrated by a keenness of observation and a subtlety of inquiry worthy of a Philo Vance or an Inspector Maigret, threw a vivid light on the old Jewish passion for the pure exercise of the intellect. And the device for getting out of besieged Jerusalem by having himself laid in a coffin, and arriving in this way at the conqueror's tent, contained multiple meanings: it denoted a taste for disguise and a macabre black humor, which did not detract from the portrait of the personage, and moreover revealed a healthy sense of reality, an instinct for survival that prevailed, despite Yochanan ben Zakkai's very advanced age, over the temptation of superfluous and altogether facile heroism. And this was a situation that sufficiently applied, willy-nilly, to the present. Its natural redemption, then, was contained in the request addressed by the venerable teacher, once he had been lifted from his coffin, to the Roman general's peasant mistrustfulness: not abstract pleas for freedom, not the restoration of a political independence now irretrievably lost and perhaps even harmful, but the insignificant concession of a small plot of land, where Yochanan himself, and a few followers as mad as himself, would be able to devote themselves to the study of the sacred texts. An almost grotesque scene, and at the same time grandiose: a little old man, with hardly any breath left in him—and one almost gets the suspicion that the business of the coffin was also a device to arouse pity—who, against the background of the apocalyptic burning of a great city, comes to ask an astonished conqueror for permission to attend to his studies. To study what? Incomprehensible stories, which allowed that most illustrious of Roman historians, the stern Tacitus, to call the civilization of the Jews "*mos absurdus sordidusque*," a mixture of the base and the unreasonable. But meanwhile it is to this strange request that we owe the contemporary world's fortune, or misfortune, of knowing the theological convictions and moral precepts by which the Jewish people, through ups and downs, has shaped its life for centuries. At the cost of a huge sacrifice, imposed on it by Yochanan ben Zakkai, and which would last until the re-establishment of the state of Israel, according to the conclusion of Giorgio's whole speech: the cost of having had, since that distant episode, the world for a homeland and their own hearts for a Temple.*

Yochanan ben Zakkai, besides being the savior of Judaism, had the single fault of being the consolidator of the Talmudic tradition, which had barely begun, and to which are due infinite refinements in exercises of intellectual acumen, collected under the name *pilpul*, which designates the art of splitting and resplitting hairs already slender enough to begin with. The Talmud and Talmudism had a staunch adversary in Martin Buber, who glorified the holy simplicity of the Hasidim, another typically Jewish form of the delirious madness to which the loving search for God can lead.

---

* What is probably the only surviving text of this memorable lecture bears a dedication to the present writer, "that in reaching the pure sources of tradition, he may gain the certainty that a world will come in which Wagner, Nietzsche, and Mendelssohn will finally be reconciled." The recipient replied with a dedication "from free man to free man"—an echo of the poet Foscolo.

Martin Buber had left traces of himself with another book, in that same dusty library, in addition to the collection of stories about the holy Baal Shem. This was a work, published in Italy as *Sette discorsi sull'ebraismo*, composed on the eve of the First World War, and disavowed by the author himself in the years of his splendid old age, which blossomed in the gardens of Zion, in the re-established Jewish state to which Yochanan ben Zakkai had attached no importance. It was a series of seven speeches, impetuous and vehement, such as may come from the pen of a young man anxious to review the whole past, to point out the mistakes of his predecessors, and to arrange the world in a definite and better way—and if this was not what he was driving at, it was certainly what his present readers wanted. Already at the beginning there were words that each of the students had for a long time addressed to himself:

"The question I put to you and myself today is the question of what meaning Judaism has for the Jews.

"Why do we call ourselves Jews? Perhaps because we really are such? And what does it mean to be a Jew? By putting this question to you today, I do not mean to speak to you of abstractions, but of your life, of our life, considered not in its external form, but in its innermost quality and living essence.

"Why do we call ourselves Jews? Only because that is what our fathers called themselves, out of an inherited custom? Or does the name have any root in reality?

"Out of inherited custom? Tradition is the noblest freedom for the generation that lives it with all its senses, but it is the most ignoble slavery for passive heirs who accept it inertly and rigidly. What meaning does it have for us, this inheritance, this name, this badge, this command: Judaism? To what kind of collectivity do we bear witness when we call ourselves Jews? What does our passage over the abyss mean? Do we fall through the fog of millennia into oblivion, or does some power bring us to the fulfillment of a destiny? What does it mean, this will of ours to preserve ourselves not only as men, human spirit, and human seed, but also—in spite of the times and time itself—as Jews?"

To these difficult questions, Buber gave an initial answer, at first sight paradoxical, but which mirrored to perfection the situation and state of mind of the small surviving fragments of Jewish unity under the sky darkened by the Hitlerite storm. It was a quotation from Moritz Heimann: "Whatever a Jew, stranded on the most isolated, inaccessible island, still recognizes as a Jewish problem, that alone is it." So persecution and the war, and total separation from what was left of the Jewish world, were the group's situation, and now it was starting to justify its presumption in confronting basic questions with such inadequate means.

But Martin Buber's encouragement went still further. He transcribed the bold words of the Baal Shem: "We say God of Abraham, God of Isaac, and God of Jacob; we do not say God of Abraham, Isaac, and Jacob. This is to tell you: Isaac and Jacob did not rely on the tradition of Abraham, but themselves sought the Divine." Thus before each person, whatever his means and situation, the opportunity opens to attempt the absurd enterprise. And it is not only a possibility, but a duty as well.

And even more audacious goals are offered by old Jewish legends, a perennial source of lofty myths and intoxicating spiritual adventures, resolved in the play, which is likewise drama, of an illuminating sentence or remark. One tells of a leprous beggar, sitting and waiting at the gates of Rome. When someone asks him what he is waiting for, the scorching reply is: you. No allowance is made for hesitations or doubts.

These premises now served to justify any bold speculation, any struggle for renewal. Buber himself was an insistent example, by reclaiming for Judaism its great glories that had been judged heretical in the course of the centuries, from Jesus, the most daring of all revolutionaries, who entrusted to man's good will the possibility of achieving the kingdom of heaven on earth, to the heroic furor of the rationalist Spinoza, who recognized the potential identity of heaven and earth— *Deus sive natura*—in the sense that the complex mystery, which we are accustomed to consider so remote from us, can be seen in every aspect and moment of daily reality.

Destructive barbs of irony were aimed at the humanitarian innovators of the nineteenth and twentieth centuries, who so easily forgot the original and proud meaning of the name Israel: he who wrestles with his Lord. The traditionalists, in their concern to safeguard the purity of the heritage of the fathers, had embalmed in a network of pedantic injunctions the fire of the burning bush, the irrepressible scorn of the prophets, and the audacities of the singers of Judah, who were on intimate terms with the Lord. But the present re- formers limited their ambition to a Judaism expounded to the people in terms of the positivist dogmas contained in popular encyclopedias. Their great battles consisted in ex- plaining the hygienic basis for the Mosaic precepts, and in promoting the replacement of classical Hebrew in the Sab- bath services by various spoken tongues in order to make Judaism more accessible.

It remained to cut down to size those who sought to nor- malize the Jewish anomaly on tne national level—the Jewish epigones of the European nationalist movement, Herzl, Pin- sker, Zangwill, and Nordau, and their contemporaries of a socialist persuasion, Gordon and Borochov. They were looked on with suffecent detachment, almost ignored. Whether they rebuilt a Jewish state or not, and whether in the image of Mazzini's Italy, Lenin's Russia, or Fabian England was of little importance. It was perhaps legitimate to concern oneself with the Jews, and with questions of how they should be organized, but the thing called Judaism, apart from the sure and absolute recognition of its identity, was the essential problem. Once it was resolved, all the rest would fall into place as a logical consequence, or better still as a side issue.

That honest and humble thinker Achad Haam, whose pseudonym is a statement in itself—it means, very simply, "one of the people"—offered a seemingly wise solution. A Jewish state, yes, but as a symbolic definition, the concrete representation of a spiritual platform (a simple tile measuring twenty square centimeters, suggested Giorgio's engineer brother). This tiny full stop would allow the Jews to develop their own aptitudes for scientific disciplines and spiritual searching; perhaps it would even allow them to experiment with new forms of social organization. A grand, noble, and at the same time petty ideal to those who had not discarded the sense of Judaism's final goal, complete redemption, the Messiah invoked by Isaiah and Jesus. All or nothing. Man and his God, in one immense, indivisible union, in accordance with the prophetic utterance: "You are my witnesses, and I am God." And in accordance with the interpretation of the mystic Shimon ben Yochai: "If you are not my witnesses, I am no longer God."

There was enough to turn the disputants into so many Hillels and Shammais, the traditional antagonists in the Talmudic tradition. All copied the intolerance of the subtle, quibbling Shammai, but all laid claim to the candor, sweetness, and dazzling capacity for intuition of Hillel. So as to have in readiness the answer he gave to a heathen who asked him to explain the Law in the time he was able to stand on only one foot: "Do not do unto others what you would not wish to have done unto you. And now go, my son. All the rest is only commentary."

The sublime simplicity of the great words destined to move the world! Today we are used to utterances of a different kind: "Drink Coca-Cola," "Make love, not war." While instead it is necessary to go back to the peremptory purity of the great moral imperatives, which gets muddied solely because of our pettifogging distinctions. While to anyone who has good will as an essential possession, how easy the road to be followed appears! It is still indicated by such clear words: do not kill, do not steal, do not bear false witness.

And yet, and yet . . . Very often, it is not we but reality itself that imposes the distinctions on us. "Do not do unto others" is a negative command that can lead, absurdly enough, to complete inaction. And its reverse, which constitutes the revolution of Jesus the Nazarene—"Do unto others as you would have them do unto you"—implies a possible violation of the freedom of others. What if the others don't like it? Tastes, as popular wisdom knows, are countless and conflicting.

Hillel's proposition is as sublime as it is utopian. Just as contingency called into question the very commandments imparted to Moses on Mount Sinai. Every day brought proof that to bear false witness could even be a heroic duty. A partisan caught by the Nazis had to conceal the truth in order to cover his comrades' tracks. And he also had to kill. In few periods of history, did killing rise, without a shadow of a doubt, to the height of a moral imperative as in the years of which we speak. It is almost always impossible to say whether a war is just or unjust, but the struggle against the monster of Hitlerism was an absolute necessity. Not to mention the fact that only in messianic times is it possible to conceive of man's survival without the sacrifice of other beings.

Thus the incivility and intolerance of Shammai, who had rudely repulsed the heathen inquirer, were unwittingly rehabilitated. Distinctions are the very life of man, they represent the curse connected with the greatest of divine gifts, thought—and with the disconcerting complexity of the environment in which we live. Man always deludes himself that he can get along with a single formula. But reality and life constantly break up before him into countless and conflicting streams. Hence the continual need to specify, order, distinguish. Only a meticulous set of precepts, case by case, can allow the application of the sublime words. Hillel himself declared that all the rest is only commentary, but he carefully avoided mentioning how long the commentary is and whether we can do without it.

Shammai and Hillel, two symbols of the Jewish adventure, but also two personifications of what is—and, we suspect, always will be—man's drama. In the presence of Hillel and Shammai, it becomes no longer a paradox but an urgent duty to adopt the attitude of the Hasid Zev Wolf of Zbarazh, unrecognized precursor of Alessandro Manzoni, at the spectacle of two quarreling men who were coming to blows. Urged to intervene, he gave this reply: "To me, they're both right, and who would dare to come between two righteous men?"

This, then, led to the ultimate truth: that the only one on the side of wrong was the policeman, who, slumped in his chair, continued imperturbably to snore. The world around him was collapsing, but he, poor devil, flung out of his native Sicily smack into the midst of the Jews, what could he do about it? His slumber looked like true and total resignation, with neither confident nor desperate expectation of any change in the present state of things. But from the standpoint of someone who has always seen things get worse, are changes really desirable? We would have to ask those two famous doctors whose names sound so strange and enigmatic—at least to those who do not know Hebrew. In translation they sound somewhat more familiar. They could be called Praise and Celestine. And Praise, or Hillel if you like, when not engaged in ideological debate, is said to have plied the trade of shoemaker.

## VII / CHARACTERS

Things were going badly for the century's children. In Africa, Rommel had blasted Auchinleck's divisions, crossed almost the whole coastal desert, and was approaching the bay of Alexandria and the Suez Canal. Unless a miracle should occur, he was on the point of cutting the West's vital supply routes. And the boundless Russian steppes likewise seemed insufficient to stem the onslaught of the Wehrmacht and its generals, Mannstein, Paulus, and Bock. Without another miracle, the fate of Stalingrad, the Russian stronghold on the Volga, appeared sealed. There was no reason to have any illusions, and no one did. Yet, strange to say, people's spirits were infinitely less troubled than the situation demanded.

Meanwhile, connections with the outside world were not entirely precluded. Above the many front lines passed reports that could not be suppressed, and this reduced the anxiety of isolation. The subdued gong beat of Radio London, even as a prelude to disastrous news, was something more than a source of information. It was the symbol of a situation that no amount of bullying would be able to change: despite everything, the civilized world was still united.

The day may come when this story of families gathered around the radio, the climate of tension, the recurrent, devouring fear that rose at the hour of rendezvous with those distant friends, will be entirely forgotten. And it will be a great pity, because future generations will be kept from understanding an important aspect of the life of that time. Or else—a more unlikely hypothesis, but not to be discarded, considering the human tendency to create legends—that gong beat will rise to the level of an almost magical symbol, a call from on high, guiding oppressed peoples in their struggle against a monstrous adversary. This too will be a pity, because legends, no matter how noble and poetic, are always a way of falsifying history. My own modest hope, almost certainly destined to be unfulfilled, would be that we be judged in the distant future for what we really were. But in the light of experience, one must say it's an impossible hope. The fault is ours, and we should have the courage to admit it. We are the only creatures, at least on this earth, who are concerned to leave evidence of themselves in time, addressed to our children's children and our remote descendants. But it is certainly easier to reconstruct the past from the petrified bone of a dinosaur than by interpreting the flattering epitaph erected in honor of a king or glorious conqueror. And one nearly insurmountable obstacle is represented by those faithful and dispassionate memoirs that every so often some sincere worthy leaves behind for the edification of future generations, and the present book is no exception. This honest intention almost always ends by reshuffling the cards and distorting the truth.

Radio London was a comfort to all anti-Fascists and neutral-minded citizens, assuming there were any left. But Monferini's students, with the spread of bad news, found just as many reasons to submerge themselves increasingly in the happy little world they had created without even realizing it. Indeed, it might be said that with the approach of the hurricane, the frivolity of the youthful company prevailed over its commitment to study and discussion. They were at the very age that demanded the elementary rights of play and joy, something these boys and girls had experienced to such a scant degree; and while it is true that front-line combat, or in any case long military service, did not hang over them, as it did over almost all their contemporaries, it should also be remembered that they were being denied a carefree student life, the innocent pleasures of informal parties, trips abroad, and romantic caprices. Above all, they could never in all those years be separated. These were things that they made a point of disparaging and deriding, for the sole purpose of concealing a deep and bitter regret.

Reactions varied and were often contradictory. In general, one was led to accentuate feverishly one's own inclinations. Roberto saw the future world more and more in terms of visual representation and the history of cinema. Aldo maintained that the only way to check something was to reduce it to its arithmetical dimension, and that the whole question could be interpreted as an architectural symbol; while his girl friend Giuliana multiplied her efforts to provide him with snacks, as often as three times a day. The Freudian behaved in the same way as the mathematician, changing only the nature of the symbol, while the literary type was led to think that everything boiled down to a correct interpretation of Kafka and Dostoevsky. As for Silvio, he squinted his near-sighted eyes and gazed at some distant point, while reeling off violent, staccato lines of verse, dazzling flashes of light that were almost incomprehensible: it would take six years to reveal their meaning. Even the skirt-chasers, the incorrigible Don Juans, were led to carry their tendencies to their ultimate, sometimes disagreeable consequences. It became increasingly difficult, almost impossible, to buy silk shirts or suits made with good fabrics. Nevertheless there were some in the group who succeeded in always looking impeccable; and Piero went so far as to drive around Rome in a fine carriage drawn by a superbly-gaited horse that ate peaches, which had to be fresh, otherwise it refused them. Handsome

Augusto, who wasn't all that handsome, kept trying to break his own record for the number of unknown women and girls he accosted on the street, but the tally never rose above the record set in the previous twenty-four hours. True, he occasionally received some resounding slaps, as occurred under the clock in the railroad station, when he asked a beautiful passerby if she could give him the correct time. But it is also true that his appeals, like the hunter's birdlime, exercised a mysterious attraction. One fine spring evening, passing a garden, he instinctively whistled in the direction of a half-open and dimly lighted window, through which no one was visible. "Is that you, Giorgio?" a woman's subdued voice called, vibrant with passion and desire. The quiver in her voice was enough to make Augusto jump over the fence. Almost immediately the light went out, and no voice or sound could be heard. The darkness had obviously caused the woman to mistake Augusto for Giorgio, or more probably had given her an excuse to find out how far the unknown seducer would carry his boldness.

Other amours were less risky and less carnal. Instead of amours, they might better be called colloquies, endless and complex colloquies—or soliloquies when, as often happened, the girl did nothing but listen. The Circolare Rossa tram was no longer the best place for such outpourings. But Rome in those days still abounded in parks and shady avenues. Automobiles, not exactly numerous before the war, had almost all disappeared: one of the very few pleasant consequences of the conflict. And thus aided by solitude and evening darkness, one young student was able to psychoanalyze his sweetheart; pleasure was combined with utility, it being the first such experiment he had performed. And the girl, angel that she was, stayed on, as no patient really in need of treatment would have done.

Another form often followed and enjoyed for its greater

possibilities of colloquy, was the foursome. The secluded Giardino del Lago and the beautiful, interminable Via Nomentana—but today it would be perfectly useless to try it again: the din of the automobiles prevents you from concentrating your thoughts, and the benches and flowerbeds have disappeared, giving way to parking spaces on the street so dear to the obscure pleasures of d'Annunzio's Andrea Sperelli—were places that particularly favored this kind of expression. Leafy trees rose above the two couples as they strolled slowly, more and more caught up in their excited chatter, which never let up but skimmed lightly and tirelessly over the analysis of conflicting reactions, preferences, and desires, and the obstacles that stood in the way of what seemed so natural and within reach; over what each one dreamed of doing, should the impossible—namely, the end of the war—take place and the outcome be favorable; over the crazy things they would be able to do, in different and inconceivable times, like eating bread made with pure flour; over the books they would read, an infinitely greater number than the few available; over the way their children, assuming they ever had any, would hear the story of this strange and emotional existence; over powerful and lucky America, which had no direct experience of the war; over the inevitable Kafka, of course; and Monferini and Buber.

Sometimes, out of an unconscious need for change, the couples would switch partners, but as in a quite natural and innocent game. It was a small drama, which barely rippled the waters. Sudden jealousies abated, and friendship and mutual trust regained the upper hand. Soon the conversation was resumed, more lively and intense than ever.

Families had become less important. This was understandable: the atmosphere at home was always one of gloomy thoughts and problems that one would have liked to forget. Some parents, worried about what seemed to them an abnormal situation, made an effort to grasp what might be the cause of tendencies so different from the traditional ones of Rome's Jewish community. But Monferini, despite the slings and arrows of Donna Maria, also knew how at the proper moment to find persuasive words of common sense. He was able to be an excellent educator, not only of children, but of their parents, when they gave him the opportunity.

He was not bothered by the friendships and discussions, nor even by the amours. "He who is alone," says the wisdom of Ecclesiastes, "how shall he warm himself?" And the cold of wartime was making itself acutely felt in both its physical and spiritual dimensions.

Monferini was concerned about a strange boy who occupied a desk by himself, still wore short pants at the age of seventeen, and never took part in the class discussions. He was obviously a problem, and in the background one could sense other problems, though it was hard to make them out.

Every morning a little group of persons caught the attention of passersby in the vicinity of Piazza Sonnino, on the edge of Trastevere. The boy walked to school followed by a younger brother and sister. All three wore the same brown jackets, and the trousers of the boys and the little girl's skirt seemed to be made of the same material. A tall man, dressed in a dark suit, brought up the rear, walking with head erect and gazing into the distance, a pose too rigid to be natural. None of the four exchanged so much as a word with the others.

It was the same in class. The boy shared neither his joys nor concerns with anyone. When questioned, he answered in a hoarse, oddly childish voice, barely loud enough to be heard by someone straining to listen, that he had done his homework. On rare occasions, reacting to some performance by Monferini or curious way of showing-off by the students, he smiled to himself, a tight, barely perceptible smile. The minute anyone noticed, took it as a hint, and tried to speak to him, the smile immediately vanished and his usual absent look reappeared. By now everyone was used to his presence, and except for Monferini, almost no one paid any attention to him.

A father's duties include keeping himself informed about his child's progress or failure in school. This boy's father was clearly a man conscious of his duty, since one day he came to consult Monferini. But he had not expected to encounter such a teacher. His long career as a magistrate—before the racial laws, he had been the most feared public prosecutor in the kingdom—had never brought him in contact with a teacher so impatient with traditional norms and customs. Moreover, since laying aside his judicial robes, he had accepted, merely as a duty, the leadership of the Jewish Community. In a certain sense, Monferini was his subordinate.

All this was enough to make Monferini forget about the son and concentrate almost exclusively on the father. It was an indictment that surpassed in violence any with which the magistrate had charged the most hardened criminals.

"I don't know you, but judging by your son's behavior, you must be a real tyrant, an unbearable dictator, at least at home. Don't start telling me your reasons, I know them already, it doesn't take any particular intelligence to see them. I'm told you're a widower, and you're probably reluctant to give your children the care and affection that a mother normally does. You think you're incapable of it, but you don't even try. And you're afraid of letting yourself go and being too indulgent, of accustoming these children to too loving an atmosphere. You worry too much about the trials they'll probably have to face, and you're inclined to underestimate their capacity to stand up to them. You try to judge them by your professional standards, which you think are objective. But a child doesn't only want to be judged, he also wants to be understood and forgiven, at least at home. He needs it as a right, he claims it as a necessity, one that under no circumstances can he do without."

Here Monferini fell silent, aware of having let himself be carried away by his anger. The fear of being driven beyond the permissible could never restrain him, but the feeling of having skirted the ridiculous, yes. What, after all, did he know of the life and concerns of the man sitting before him?

The man sitting before him, with eyes upturned and lips scornfully closed, continued to stare at some indefinable point in the room.

Suddenly he stood up and started toward the door, which opened on the corridor. Having reached it, and without even turning around or lowering his head for a single moment, he said in a loud, ringing voice: "I thank you, Professor Monferini. From the bottom of my heart."

From that day on, the boy participated more in the life of the school, which doesn't mean he was any happier. But a few months later, his father, as president of the Community, had to face the most arduous trial of his career as a magistrate and a man. With the German occupation of Rome, he found himself face to face with those who were demanding, in exchange for the promised safety of the Community in his charge, the payment of fifty kilos of gold objects.

He handled the matter with great dignity and no illusions. He thanked the Vatican authorities, who had discreetly informed him that, if need be, they would intervene. But he preferred that the Jews of Rome pay out of their own pockets, while looking the odious extortioners straight in the eye. He insisted on being present when the objects were delivered and weighed, stubbornly disputing fraudulent attempts to tip the scales. Meanwhile, he and some trusted and heroic associates hid the Community's real treasures in a safe place: the fine fabrics, the silver objects imbued with Jewish and Roman history, the manuscripts and incunabula from the library. Not to mention, of course, the sacred scrolls of the Torah.

Then he remained undaunted, his eyes looking straight ahead, awaiting the tragedy that he knew could not be averted. When it came, he did his utmost to warn the scattered members of the Community, to console those about to be deported, and to organize the first contacts and assistance among the survivors. He did not let himself be caught, as he was certainly inclined to do, since he felt he had not yet done his entire duty.

In the months that followed, without once sparing himself, he found time to think of those who would come later and probably refuse to believe what had happened. Mindful that in the wave of emotion of those who have seen and suffered, there is a human tendency to distort facts, he compiled an official report on what had taken place. It lists names, supplies numbers, and describes episodes, all without comment. This document constitutes still today the most convincing testimony on the roundup and deportation of more than a thousand Roman Jews, which occurred at dawn on October 16, 1943. It is a crushing denunciation, uttered before the tribunal of history by a public prosecutor who, in the exercise of his office, had long learned to set aside feelings and resentment.

Anyone wishing to see evidence of the man's feelings will find it on the back wall of the small museum set up in the Temple on the Lungotevere Cenci, to house the furnishings and ornaments saved by President Ugo Foà. It is a leaf from a calendar, now under glass, bearing that date of October 16, and with these two words jotted underneath in a firm hand: "German infamy." Nothing more.

# VIII / IN UTROQUE IURE

Even skeptics are sometimes led to speak of miracles. In the years since the war, specialists in military history have been laboring to show that Rommel's supply lines would not have allowed him to advance more than a meter beyond El Alamein, and that a thousand square meters of soil sufficed for the Russian defenders to halt the German armies on the Volga. All this gets demonstrated with charts and figures, though it's still hard to explain why the German General Staff had not foreseen the limits placed on its advances, and why they halted precisely at those very points beyond which the strategic perspective of the war underwent a radical and probably decisive about-face. In any case, the military history specialists have considered the problem *afterwards*, with documents and analyses at their disposal, but *at the time* people were more prone to speak of miracles and heave a long-suppressed sigh of relief. After El Alamein and Stalingrad, history began to march the other way, and this happened with a sudden rapidity that no untrained spectator could have expected. Through the first rift in the clouds one glimpsed the coming end of the storm, and people's thoughts quite naturally turned to what tomorrow held in store once fine weather had come back. For the moment, they were concerned primarily with survival, and with holding in check their impatience, an inner adversary that kept pawing the ground.

In the span of three years of war—the exact duration of the *liceo*—the students had been growing up. Now they were faced with the problem of continuing their studies, so as to be ready for the moment when they might re-enter civic life. But circumstances did not allow anyone to follow his preferences and inclinations. In itself, it was an arduous, not to say impossible, task to launch such a restricted group in university studies. And yet something was done; indeed, two paths—or two choices—opened before those who were qualified. And some who were more eager than others tried their best to pursue both, thus prompting Giorgio to croon in his usual way:

> Son Pereda, son ricco d'onore,
> baccelliere me fe' Salamanca;
> sarò presto *in utroque* dottore,
> chè di studi ancor poco mi manca.

The Pontificium Institutum Utriusque Iuris, next to the Lateran Basilica, opened its doors to Jewish students interested in the field of jurisprudence. It was a rather unusual school, international in character, like the one that drew young priests and seminarians from all over the world, isolating them from the war in the extraterritorial colleges of Rome. It was a first, exciting opportunity offered by the Roman pope to Jewish students, descendants of those whom one of his predecessors, in 1555, contravening an age-old tradition of tolerance, had confined within the walls of the ghetto. The Lateran, moreover, offered itself as the only Roman university institution where, in those days, there was almost complete freedom of speech. It was not out of caution, but by tradition, and to overcome the Babel of many tongues, that Latin was spoken almost exclusively. A rather odd Latin, which took on rapid-fire rhythms in the Spanish accent of the then Monsignor Larraona, a keen and bewildering lecturer on Roman law, or bristled with neologisms in the speech of the Reverend Father De Schepper, a Belgian Capuchin in his eighties, venerable, gentle, and serene, who taught political (or rather *socialis*) economy, infinitely oblivious to the restlessness of his students. He would discourse on *marxiana doctrina* with the same fondness and detachment that he might have reserved for the hagiography of the early Christian martyrs. But when the then Monsignor Staffa, standing erect in all his imposing bulk, one hand under his cassock, which he wore like a toga, and the other lifted high in a gesture that reminded you of Cicero, began to speak of matters so remote as those related to canon law, his listeners leaned forward attentively: in his voice resounded the tone of the compilers of the Decretals. And when Monsignor Perugini, secretary of Pontifical Briefs and Letters, crouching in his armchair, expatiated on the subject of international juridical problems facing the Church, there hovered in the classroom the methods and the very spirit of Livy and Tacitus, no longer names lost in time, but realities still to be felt in our present, and certainly in the distant future as well, whatever many people nowadays may think.

Latin, especially during exams, represented a problem, but one that was not all that serious. And besides, in a youthful environment, there are other decisive elements that help to overcome the difficulties of acclimatization. There is friendship, so easy to establish among those who know little of yesterday's troubles but think instead of tomorrow. And there is curiosity, to propel spirits still tireless and unafraid of disappointment.

With Father Arcangelo, a young Tuscan Servite, this happened with particular ease. Those on the Jewish side were looking upward to a total renewal of the world and man; as for him, he had set himself a more concrete but no less ambitious goal. He dreamed of becoming pope, and said so with a disarming candor that matched his name. On these premises, it was more than natural to exchange books, opinions, and experiences. It seemed quite obvious that by realizing both ambitions, useful contacts would be established on both the temporal and spiritual levels. Meanwhile, one was happy to laugh, as one's age allowed, at the Latin neologisms coined in the Lateran classrooms. Some were ingenious, others frankly ridiculous. Nevertheless they represented not only the fruit of the love for a language that ecclesiastical tradition has never considered dead—now this is happening, and many are sincerely sorry—but also, it should not be forgotten, a compelling necessity.

From the Vatican to Fribourg in Switzerland: international connections were expanding. Fribourg was the label that guaranteed to another, more substantial group of Jewish boys the possibility of pursuing their studies in the more arduous field of mathematics and the physical sciences, in order to become tomorrow's engineers. But in reality it was something much larger and more important, which the name of the Swiss city furnishing the label for that course of studies does not reveal, as can be seen from a meticulous report on its laborious beginnings that has only recently come to light:

"Following the announcement that the Institut Technique Supérieur of Fribourg (Switzerland) was accepting the enrollment of young Italians without requiring their attendance, there arose in October 1941 the idea of instituting in Rome courses to prepare for the examinations of the said Institute, courses that could be taken by young people of the Jewish race, who due to the racial laws were not admitted to our universities.

"Having been invited to coordinate these courses, I saw immediately that the said Institute bore a greater resemblance to our professional schools than to a university faculty.

I therefore thought it advisable to give our courses a much higher aim, equivalent to that on which instruction in the first two years of our science faculties (engineering candidates) is based.

"This for various reasons. In the first place, it was desirable that students enrolled in these courses be able to enter the corresponding level in the university on the day when the racial laws would be abolished.

"Secondly, one could always hope that the students themselves would be accepted at the major Swiss Polytechnic Schools, which offer a higher curriculum than Fribourg. Last but not least, I considered it advisable that highly gifted students, above average in their education, should be able to enjoy the beauties of pure science, without the limitations imposed by narrowly professional instruction; and I thought that these young people, unjustly hindered in their aspirations by the racial laws, would find consolation and feel their spirits raised by coming to grips with the problems of modern science.

"My ideas were accepted by an administrative committee headed by S.E. Almansi, president of the Union of Israelite Communities.

"The committee entrusted me with the responsibility of organizing the courses and choosing the teachers. This latter task was not easy, since I could not have recourse only to coreligionists, and also had to choose from among Aryan teachers individuals sympathetic to the plight in which the students found themselves. I must say immediately that in this respect as well the teachers named below understood the importance of the mission entrusted to them.

"The courses began on December 1, 1941, with 25 students, under the title *Coordinating Courses in Mathematics*.

"The curriculum was set up by the teachers with my approval, keeping in mind the university programs offered in the first two years of Engineering. I followed the progress of the courses day by day, and conducted several classes myself; complementary ones in the History of Mathematics were given by Prof. F. Enriques.

"At the end of the scholastic year 1941-42, I monitored all the examinations and had the pleasure of noting the brilliant results obtained by students who had carried out studies while in a particularly painful state of mind.

"Of 25 students, judged by the same criteria adopted in university examinations, 19 obtained marks in all subjects of not less than 24, and of these, 12 had marks of not less than 27.

"Given the success of the first course, a second course was instituted in the scholastic year 1943-44.

"This second course was pursued by the students with the same zeal and interest as the first, and the results of the examinations held last June were excellent.

"I should mention here that, at our request, the Ecole d'Ingénieurs in Lausanne, an excellent Swiss polytechnic school, allowed the enrollment in the second year (equivalent to our 3rd year of Engineering) of students who had taken our courses, with the single stipulation that during the first semester of 1943-44 up there they must take a certain number of examinations; and most of the students would have accepted this solution if the hardships stemming from the war and the transfer of funds had not hindered their going abroad, and if the events of last July [i.e., the dismissal of Mussolini] had not made the students themselves hope for a solution more in keeping with the intensity of their feelings as Italians.

"I should further add that in 1942-43 a new first course was also given for students who had just graduated from high school, with the same subjects, the same programs, and the same teachers as the previous first course.

"This new first course was attended by some fifteen pupils, some from other cities.

"In conclusion, there emerge today from the *Coordinating Courses in Mathematics* some twenty students prepared to enter the third year of Engineering (first year at the university level), one candidate to enter the third year for the degree in mathematics, and some ten prepared for the second year of the Faculty of Sciences (engineering candidates).

"These students, notwithstanding the state of mind under which they pursued their studies, have nevertheless, by the zeal they demonstrated and the ability of their teachers, acquired a preparation equivalent to that of corresponding university students. Of this equivalence, especially for the subjects in my particular field, I can give absolute assurance.

"I should only point out that so as not to depart too widely from the curricula of the Swiss polytechnic schools, the second year saw the introduction of the Science of Constructions (elements), which in Rome is studied in the third year (first year of the faculty of Engineering), and two general courses were omitted, in Mineralogy and Geology, and in Technology, which in Rome are covered in the first two years.

"These gaps, similar to those shown by students coming from other universities, can easily be filled.

"Taking into consideration all the circumstances explained above, I believe that the young people of whom I speak deserve to be admitted to the third year and respectively to the second year of the University of Rome (Faculty of Engineering and Science), where, I have no doubt, they will show how diligently they have studied and the profit they have thereby derived.

"Rome, September 1943"

These words were written by one of the leading mathematicians of modern Italy, which, in recognition of his great merit, made him a senator for life. Guido Castelnuovo was of such stature that in those days he could reply to a student who asked him to explain Einstein's intuitions: "You must excuse me, but it's really impossible. There are only two or three of us in Italy at the present moment who have understood anything about it." But he did not refuse, in the moment of need, to concern himself with calculations rather more petty than the kind to which he was accustomed, and perhaps more complicated to resolve, like the economic problems related to the course he had been assigned.

At his side was another renowned figure in Italian and world science, Federigo Enriques, who was his brother-in-law, and though himself a mathematician, more inclined to philosophy. The course he gave in the history of mathematics was a memorable event, and drew not only engineering students. The handsome old man and charming gentleman who ascended the platform as though it were his throne, and with a regal gesture laid down a pair of ever new and impeccable pigskin gloves, spoke with the soft, direct voice of the great persuaders. He led his listeners to a clear comprehension of complex relationships, to a singling out of hitherto unsuspected connections. In his explanation, the entire history of the world, apart from the civic, moral, and ideological aspects and hues that we are accustomed to recognizing in it, took the form of a ceaseless effort to understand the absolute relations, most certainly of a mathematical kind, that govern its seemingly tumultuous course.

Along with these two great men, there were other teachers whose task it was to handle basic subjects. Guido Castelnuovo had immediately thought of two men who for a great many years had worked as his assistants. Though they were not Jews, they responded at once to the appeal of their friend and teacher. The political aspect of the problem did not bother them, or it may even have been a strong incentive.

Besides, they found themselves working with esteemed colleagues, and teaching students endowed with enormous strength of will.

Giulio Bisconcini was—and still is today, in his marvelously ardent old age—an indefatigable little man, who in order to explain his subject had to be in constant motion. His frantic restlessness was a stimulus to everyone, and they recognized him above all as a noble and understanding friend.

But a figure still closer to the students—not for nothing was he a friend of Monferini to the end of his days—was the other assistant, Professor Lucaroni. Professor in a manner of speaking: Raffaele Lucaroni was always the staunch enemy of academic titles and careers, oaths and administrative ties, to the point that having spent his entire existence in the classrooms of Italian universities, he lived out his long and tranquil old age to the moment of death without receiving so much as a crumb of pension.

He was from the Marches, by origin, by inclination, by emotional attachment. HIs father was a longshoreman, and his older brother, a simple newspaper vendor, had supported him during his education. According to legend, he had taken part in Ancona's famous "Red Week." Not as a socialist, of course: he considered socialism an ideological dogma, just barely tolerable in a phase of mutual cooperation. Himself, he was an anarchist, a true exponent of anarchism in its Italian manifestation. And his ideas had been clear in his head for a very long time.

". . . You, who uphold nonexistent political freedoms, why instead don't you join all those who struggle to have greater ones that would allow the participation in lawmaking by all the people, who only then will be responsible for naming their representatives?

"At this point our adversaries get angry and say: if today one were to give more political freedoms to the people, they wouldn't know how to govern themselves and would lose their independence by fighting among themselves. . . .

"All right then, it's true, the Italian citizen is ignorant. And when do you propose to take him out of his ignorance?

"You say that with courage he'll be able to do it; but as far as one can see, the elevation of the people by your efforts comes rather late, because if you really had faith in the progress of the people, you would already have begun to make the elementary schools truly compulsory; you would have reduced or removed indirect taxes on such prime necessities as bread, salt, pasta, coffee, etc., and increased them for luxury goods that serve only for the rich and not the poor; you would have reduced the money spent on the army and spent more on agriculture; and thus we would have active citizens and prosperity in this country, things that can only favor progress.

"But until you on your side do not provide education and prosperity for the people, and do not grant more political freedoms, we can hardly believe you to be lovers of Progress and Civilization."

The article from which this quotation is taken bears the terse and belligerent title "Refutation." It was published in *Il Cigno*, an anarchist newspaper of the Marches, on November 18, 1900, with this brief editorial note: "We are pleased to publish the above article, in the form in which it was submitted to us, since it is written by a lad just over thirteen years of age, who in his hours outside school applies himself to the study of social problems, and would like on this occasion to become our special contributor. And he has done so with great simplicity as well as considerable precision, something that many know-it-alls of the ruling classes might well envy."

Raffaele Lucaroni, teacher of analytical geometry, was thus a longtime anarchist, but when he was in a good mood he was willing to debate the socialists. The old surviving resi-

dents of the Via Cola di Rienzo still remember three inseparable figures who used to stroll back and forth along the
street, from the Piazza del Risorgimento to the Ponte della
Regina, again and again, until the small hours of the morning.
It was Professor Lucaroni arguing with Alceste Della Seta,
former Socialist deputy to the Italian Parliament, and now in
forced retirement after endless battles in the Chamber and
on the streets of Rome. For the latter, moreover, it was practically his fate to end up in the thick of the fray, or even to be
trampled by his adversaries; he was so nearsighted that when
fists started flying, he instantly lost his eyeglasses. I almost
forgot to say that the third member of the inseparable little
group was the friendly policeman from the local station,
whose job it was to keep tabs on these two subversives.

Another great friend of Lucaroni's, whom the students
would meet later, was Ezio Taddei. He too was an anarchist,
but with a different background. Long years of residence in
America had conditioned his way of doing things, and perhaps his literary inclinations, but not his thinking and old
habits. One could imagine him approaching the great indus-
trial colossus with more scorn than curiosity, looking only for
the best place to plant a bomb. Behind his broad, powerful
forehead one divined childish thoughts of a crystalline purity:
like those of Lucaroni. To find them together you had to
scour the cheap taverns where from time to time, in this
stifling and bureaucratic Rome, it is still possible to enjoy
shellfish. And the aroma of the sea, in addition to their attachment to ideas, was the dream that united the two men,
who had come to the capital from the two seacoasts, which
they never forgot, the Tyrrhenian and the Adriatic.

Lucaroni and Taddei were often accompanied by another
inspired madman, Roberto Secondari, a lawyer of considerable renown, but chiefly a student of animal psychology, albeit with few followers. Whatever he stated was expressed

with full and absolute certainty. The reason why cats, horses, or even animals more difficult to observe such as the snow leopard or the orangutan of Borneo, moved in certain ways was no mystery to him. But he was especially keen on explaining the profound motivations that impel dogs to lift their hind legs and piss with such frequency: on this he would have built, had the world cared to listen, a new and highly original theory of universal history, from prehistoric times to the present war.

Unfortunately, he had few listeners, and at times only Lucaroni. But Lucaroni had a sublime gift, one that made him almost godlike: he could listen intently for hours, for whole days, without paying attention to a single word of what his interlocutor was saying. Then if he looked gloomy, distracted by heaven knows what other thoughts, it was a sure sign that he was following what was being said, even with deep interest. It was a symptom that some deep impulse to contradict was ripening within him, a premonition of his imminent outburst: "So? What do you mean by that?"

When Lucaroni exploded, there were moments of bewilderment: it was so hard to know what had prompted his scorn. These were the storms that called for the peaceful intervention of Natalina, his beloved and inseparable companion. Only she could understand what was bubbling in that head of ruffled gray hair. She could understand, and even tremble at the memory, for it appeared that in his youth Lucaroni had been a dashing, irresistible Don Juan, and that his bright blue eyes had had the power to move the hearts of many women.

These were the lessons and examples, in addition to dissertations on geometry, that Raffaele Lucaroni offered his students. They might seem like small things, of little importance. But the strength of a word, of an education in feelings, is measured not by its specific importance, on which opinions can always differ, but by the mark it leaves on minds and hearts. Lucaroni was the purest of men, completely incorruptible, who shone like a luminous certainty in the gray and endless days of oppression.

During the German occupation of Rome, the son of his great friend and teacher entrusted to him, as though to a bank in Lausanne or Geneva, the bank notes that constituted the family's modest fortune. When, after the Liberation, Lucaroni returned them, he pointed out with legitimate pride the hiding place he had chosen. He had put them in the glass shade of a lamp on his desk. Had anyone pressed the switch, they would have been clearly visible, not to mention the danger of their being set on fire by the heat of the lamp. But what did a man like Lucaroni, from anarchist Ancona in the Marches, have to fear? His house was the constant refuge for antiFascists and others sought by the SS. There were so many reasons why the police should have taken an interest in that nest of subversion that it would have been all too naive of them to hope to find their prey there. In fact, during the whole Nazi occupation, none of them ever set foot inside it. Nor was there ever even a short circuit, which there would have been every reason to expect. But, in this regard, it is quite out of place to speak of miracles: many people remember how frequently power failures occurred in those days all over the city.

# IX / SNIPPETY SNAP, LIKE A PAIR OF SCISSORS

The waters were receding in a raging torrent. Man on earth is never able to perceive what is going on just below the surface. He recognizes neither the speed nor the motions of the current. The year before, a Nazi victory had seemed certain and impending; now for just the last two months, Hitler's defeat appeared certain, even imminent. Once again it was a question of waiting.

This business of waiting, and the expedients employed to pass the time, call for a word of explanation. Otherwise certain undertakings and states of mind cannot be justified.

Jotted down on a scrap of paper surviving from those days is this quotation, whose author, try as one might, is still unidentified:

*Finis totius et partis est removere viventes in hac vita de statu miseriae, et perducere ad statum felicitatis. Genus vero philosophiae sub quo hic in toto et parte proceditur, est morale negotium, sive ethica; quia non ad speculandum, sed ad opus inventum est totum et pars.*

(The whole and partial purpose is to remove those living in this life from a state of misery and lead them into a state of happiness. The kind of philosophy under which this wholly and partially takes place is a moral matter or ethics; because the whole and the part do not aim at speculating but at finding the thing to do.)

What could have led one to transcribe these words in those very days? One can only venture a guess. To remove oneself from the misery of the present to attain a happiness never before savored, that of security and the possibility of a future, is a quite understandable goal, and does not need Latin to be expressed. But to put aside pure speculation, something almost obligatory, in order to *invenire opus*, is an impulse arising from much deeper and more complex subsoil.

An example often proposed by Giorgio in the course of his furious battles with nonreligious metaphysicians comes back to mind. To what can the world be compared? To a wardrobe more than two meters high on top of which someone has placed a jar of jam. Down below, stands a little boy—mankind—longing to reach that delicious goal. According to the crude positivist, the jar will sooner or later, by some sudden agitation and the force of gravity, fall to the floor. According to the religious man, the boy's father will come along and give him the jam. While according to the imaginative idealist, the boy will grow until he is able to reach out and take possession of the prize. Now, with the help of Kafka and the times, one was beginning to suspect that the jar was empty, and that the boy would never grow tall enough to find out.

Even the strict and logical Giorgio in those months wrote verses, which are not all that bad when reread on the yellowed paper where they have remained to this day; even if the emotion of rediscovering them somewhat dims one's aesthetic sense.

> In the scenic space between clouds
> the moon is diffused

in countless opaque rays

The drifting stars
dream of strange worlds

In the fields darkened by night
houses and trees stand out
in harsh silhouette

My tortured thoughts struggle to rise
and against the clouds, low and vaporous,
that fill the valley
                                    they break
                        But hope remains.

That winter Giorgio often kept silent about the subjects close to his heart, and preferred to dwell on the poems of Eugenio Montale, whom he had just discovered.

Often I met the evil of living:
it was the choked stream that gurgles,
it was the shriveling of the parched leaf,
it was the bludgeoned horse.

Good I knew not, except for the omen
that discloses divine Indifference:
it was the statue in the slumbering noon,
and the cloud, and the soaring hawk.

This stark epitaph came up again and again in daily conversations. Which is understandable. Somewhat more difficult to perceive, across the barrier of time, is the particular meaning and importance that other utterances took on. "Bring me the sunflower maddened with sun." "Under the arcades in Modena, a liveried servant led two jackals on a leash." "Nothing makes up for the tears of the child whose balloon has escaped over the houses." "And it was mine, and it was ours, your sweet ignorance." The lines of true poets have this distinguishing feature, they can be appropriated by everyone and connected to the most unlikely circumstances.

Giorgio was not the only one to discover a poetic vocation. But the others, perhaps out of a greater sense of their limitations, or an inability to look inward, turned their energies elsewhere. Their *opus inventum*, the thing they found to take up what they thought would be the last year of the war, was putting on a musical revue. The justifications for such a crazy project have been given above, but perhaps it is unnecessary to look for any. They decided on it for no real reason, unmindful of the difficulties that would emerge along the way. The most logic and desirable hope was that their project would all too quickly prove to be unfeasible. But that was not to be.

It was easy enough to find a vehicle. Virtually anything from the sum of human knowledge lay open to them. The choice fell on a short book published in those years, a modern adaptation of Homer: Christopher Morley's *The Trojan Horse*.

Once the theme had been found, there were other matters to be resolved. Actors had to be found. But this was no problem. Practically everyone stepped forward. And there were ways to use the whole crew of volunteers, including the sports enthusiasts, who had no other interest but soccer and boxing: they were assigned to the chorus line to do the cancan. The only one left out was Giorgio, although he too had volunteered. Actually his name was discussed, along with that of his engineer brother, for the crucial task of prompter, but it was his brother who was picked, as being easier to get along with. And this suggests, in looking back, that the rejection of Giorgio was not accidental but contained an element of revenge.

While everyone could pretend to be an actor or writer,

there was one field that required genuine competence: music. Someone, by pure chance, came up with the name of Gino, the director of the Temple choir, older than all the students, already married, and the father of a little girl. Of course, it was unthinkable that Gino would neglect his choir and the thankless job of selling straw handbags on the street by which he supported his family.

But Maestro Gino accepted. Those who had felt intimidated by his exceptional height, and the exaggerated gestures of his arms in coordinating the chorus, were proved wrong. Gino had suffered more than others from the solitude of those years. He loved the company of men and women, but above all of young people. He perpetually loved to joke. His favorite joke was to give full vent to his instinctively romantic nature, and then laughingly turn it back on himself in caricature. He was a born musician, but he would have liked to express all the emotions connected with music; his dream was to play Renato or the perfidious Iago on the stage. Fortunately, he could foresee the laughter that would greet such an appearance.

The revue gave him the opportunity to realize many of his secret aspirations. Meanwhile, the musical assignment allowed him to exercise his taste for subtle imitation, for polite mockery directed chiefly at himself. Some of his compositions, more or less serious in intent, furnished the material for lively parodies; sometimes he had simply to make a few small changes in the instrumentation. But not even the classics were spared: Donizetti, Verdi, Beethoven himself.

Like a true actor, he watched for the effect of his devices on his audience. A titter, any sign of interest or involvement, showed him he was on the right track. If there was no response, he felt a pang, but the false path he had taken was forever abandoned. For him it was important to feel surrounded by people and warmth, something most helpful to the artist, or the actor on the stage. And now there was no lack of warmth.

Almost every day, until late evening, the students gathered around him to practice the difficult art of singing. What's more, he maintained that anybody, or almost anybody, can sing if he wants to: the important thing is to overcome the obstacle of feeling embarrassed at the thought that others are listening. To prove this assertion, but chiefly to bolster his secret vocation, Gino ventured day by day into a field that had never been his own: he found himself transformed into an actor. And what a magnificent actor! No costume, no gag, no gesture seemed to him inappropriate or excessive if it served the purpose of amusing the audience. To the surprise of many, he stood ready with enthusiasm to take on the role of a noble father, and even a Spanish bullfighter. His good cheer, so sincere and obliging, overwhelmed everyone and would also overwhelm the audience.

Here was a real problem. Would the show, now off to such a good start, ever find an audience? And where would it find a stage?

In the middle of the war, with Axis defeats now a daily occurrence, it was inconceivable that a group of Jews should ask the authorities for permission to put on a show. By the time anyone thought of this aspect, preparations were well along.

The theater was in bad straits, but not matrimony, apart from the fact that a great many young men found themselves on the various battlefields; but the authorities, committed to upholding the demographic policy of the regime, smoothed away difficulties in such cases. As for the Jews, who were denied the honor of bearing arms, they could still easily get married. In other words, Jewish or not, all you needed was the will.

A friend mentioned the coincidence of his sister's impending wedding. The reception would be a wartime one, but all the same there would be guests. Why not put on the revue as entertainment? This wedding was the revue's salvation. It turned it into a concrete project, with a specified opening night.

The script began to take on order and consistency. It had started from a kind of Anglo-Saxon humor, full of classical references, which are the source on which Italian students generally draw. Soon other elements appeared, to be exploited for laughs. The discovery of Roman dialect, its speech and poetry, probably occurred in these days.

Cesare Pascarella's work was highly popular among Rome's Jewish families, for its bold colors and the flavor, derived from the theater, of its principal scenes. But also, and perhaps even more, for the Risorgimento vein that ran through it, with a few pinches of mannered—and thereby considered especially biting—anticlericalism. The poems in *Villa Gloria* and *La Scoperta dell'America*, generally recited in the family from memory, had enriched many domestic vocabularies with axioms and proverbs. "The priest?—that knave has always been the enemy of patriotism and progress," Giorgio liked to quote, as his interest in religious matters gradually broadened. And he also found solid support there for his intolerance: "What is principle I respect, but what is man I trample on." As for the other Roman-dialect poet, Trilussa, who was still alive, he enjoyed even greater popularity because of his veiled anti-Fascism.

But the students, in their historical and critical research, motivated besides by a growing populism, now went back even further, bypassing the rather bourgeois, watered-down conventionality of Pascarella's and Trilussa's dialect. They rediscovered Belli—that is to say, more violent and outspoken emotions, expressed in a completely vulgar idiom—and his humble but not unworthy follower Crescenzo Del Monte, who had gathered the poor flowers of language that had grown out of the mire of the old Roman ghetto.

Belli's poems were not available to everyone. In no bookstore did you find the so-called complete edition, which had been out of print for many years. In bookstalls you might sometimes come across a bowdlerized, unreliable collection, always incomplete. At home, in some hidden nook where books that children were not supposed to read were kept, was the famous "sixth volume," in which the chaste Morandi had collected the sonnets judged most obscene, thereby achieving the opposite effect, that of offering them in their entirety to enthusiasts of this genre. Belli's true and great poetry, the polemical force of his invective, directed above all at the worst manifestations of the declining temporal papacy, his call to recover Christ in the despair of the poor, his tragic sense of life and its inseparable companion, death, his highly attuned ear for living speech, which is full and bodily substance and becomes poetry almost unawares, had still to be found and understood, but the arduous discovery almost made the students forget Cesare Pascarella's romantic oleographs and Trilussa's tame satire.

Crescenzo Del Monte's sonnets, unlike Belli's, could be found in almost every Jewish household in Rome. Their dialect, which had also been the slang of wholesale and retail merchants in large areas of the city, for both Christians and Jews, was still spoken by older family members and at least partly understood by their children. They now felt a strange pride in going back to the almost always humble origins of their families, and in grasping, in the present situation, the motives of instinctive defense and attachment to traditions that over the centuries had created this strange idiom. They discovered why their grandparents used the word *Carovve* to designate Jesus: the Hebrew *karov*, which means kinsman, is charged with fond but substantial irony. And they also learned why, in many shops, *dare una maccà* was equivalent to the Roman expression *dare una fregatura* (to cheat): the reference to the plagues of Egypt ennobled this sly bit of slang with history. There was also the word *negro*, which Jews not only in Rome but all over Italy used to designate an individual particularly doomed, by his own nature, to fail in whatever he did. It came from the Spanish meaning and spread to Italy after the expulsion of the Jews from Spain in 1492; to the Sephardic refugees it meant "unlucky," as distinguished from *moro*, meaning "melancholy." With its nouns, *negrigura* and *negrura*, and the retrograde translation into Hebrew, *shakhor*, it became in time an essential, irreplaceable element in the spoken language, and not only at home. The story is told of the remark made by the Venetian Luigi Luzzatti, famous Italian statesman and prime minister, in noting the predicament of a speaker stumbling to find words for the incompetence and mediocrity of his opponent. "He'd like to say *negro*," he was heard to mutter, "but he can't!" It was obvious that the speaker had never frequented Italian Jewish circles.

Gino was especially delighted with these little discoveries and anecdotes. Not only his situation in Rome, but also his Tuscan background, allowed him to come up with pearls whose existence had not even been suspected. Many remember the visible pleasure he showed when he had a chance to characterize two students who were constantly quarreling: "Snippety snap, like a pair of scissors—that's what you are." He went on to explain that he had gleaned this expression from a very old aunt of his.

He immediately apologized and resumed the rehearsal. By now he had fulfilled his dream and become absolutely the central figure in the whole show, so much so that another pianist had to be found to accompany the songs. One was found in the person of the engineer's recent bride. Above all there was the duet, on which Gino and everyone else had set their hearts. It was a parody sung to the tune of the overture to Donizetti's *Don Pasquale*. Gino appeared as a skinny bull-fighter, panting with love for a beautiful but unresponsive lady, played by his brother-in-law.

Donizetti's torrent of melody was an excuse, during conversations at the end of the rehearsal, to examine how music, when it emerges so completely and felicitously, determines text and situations by itself: the libretto of *Don Pasquale* is one of the best in nineteenth-century Italian opera. Compared with Elizabethan England, the France of Molière, and the Russia of Stanislavski and Chekhov, Italy has never had a great theatrical tradition. Or rather, it has had one, but not on the stages where historians are accustomed to looking. Its truest and greatest dramatists have been Donizetti, Bellini, and especially Verdi, who sometimes even sacrificed the melody for a purely theatrical effect. The discussion shifted to *Traviata* and *Rigoletto*. The "round-trip" romanza, as Gino called it, the famous passage *"Di Provenza il mare e il suol,"* is certainly not Verdi's best, but is justified by its portrayal of the character's hypocrisy, unctuousness, and false bourgeois morality, and even by his lack of imagination. The vulgarity of the finale of the third act of *Rigoletto*, the famous invective *"Sì, vendetta,"* shouted by the hunchback, is redeemed by the dramatic intensity of the situation (the revue, however, included a parody of the monologue *"Quel vecchio maledivami,"* and Rigoletto was turned into a soccer referee).

The discussion went on to *Nabucco*, whose theatrical requirements appeared contaminated by the bad taste of the period, its weakness for intrigue and amorous passions. But it was enough for the inspiration of poet and composer to turn to the prime source of the drama, the Bible, for everything to be suddenly uplifted. In the famous chorus, which even in the theater constitutes an imposing sculptural ensemble, there is almost all the power and aching beauty of Psalm

137, from which it derives; all that is missing is the desperate ferocity with which the Jewish people looked on their oppressors, a ferocity not perhaps commendable, and nevertheless justified in the light of events in twentieth-century Europe. Thus the remote tragedy of the Babylonian exile, the more recent one of the struggle for Italian independence, and the present one, against a monster destined to overshadow the deeds of any of his predecessors (about the future it is best not to make pronouncements), come together in the universal moments of human expression: music and poetry.

At this moment Gino sat down at the piano, once again the true and sensitive artist he was. He intoned one of the loveliest passages from Verdi's *Nabucco*, the solemn priestly invocation *"Tu sul labbro dei veggenti."* In the slow unfolding of the bass voice the tones of the ancient prophets came back to life; in the dark tremor of the cellos, accompanying and closing this prayer, one recognized the same mysterious and elusive melody of history.

There was the danger of neglecting the goal that had already been agreed on. It was there, however, as was the commitment, and not only to themselves, to meet it. As opening night approached, the pace of rehearsals became frantic, and other heavy duties of a physical kind were added. Some dusty old lumber, left over from the stage for a school play, was found in a basement. On wobbling tricycles, the actors transported these splintery boards to the house of their generous host. In the splendid drawing room with its antique works of art, they became carpenters and reassembled the old stage against a back wall. Curtains, expensive ones, were provided, and the bridegroom, who was a fairly good painter, painted over the joints in the boards and even sketched the scenery.

The atmosphere of the city was marked by nervous tension. Radio London, which everyone by now listened to, was announcing overwhelming victories of the Allies on both the Russian and African fronts. A great many young men, on both sides, were paying with their lives the price of a peace that at last appeared possible. But these were sacrifices that were taking place far away, and whose pitiful reality no one was able to perceive. Those who had been excluded from the struggle, through no fault of their own, were getting ready for the imminent return of the troops. Soon, very soon, the Jewish youngsters would also be lining the streets. They were under the illusion that they would be doing so with joy.

Despite all the obstacles, the revue was staged. Gino was the star of the evening, along with an attractive young singer with a vibrant voice named Giacometta, who was making her debut. It was a sure bet that once the war was over, she would be a public success as well. The climax, as anticipated, came with the final duet, and especially the singing, to Donizetti's melody, of words that had become almost the banner of the group and which expressed its rather selfish aspirations—but it seemed so daring to look beyond . . .

> For the love that's a throb
> of the whole universe,
> for that spasm sublime,
> we couldn't care less.
>
> Our love is a throb
> in only our hearts,
> wish us something better,
> and you can drop dead. . .

A throng of relatives and friends, relieved for a few hours of their persistent anxiety, came and perhaps enjoyed themselves. This last detail, however, is not all that clear, even in the memory of the participants themselves. Whether they had entertained or bored the audience was not for them a major consideration. What counted was to have experienced the weeks and months that had gone into the marvelous adventure of preparing the revue. To have participated, to have felt alive, despite everything. This, in the final analysis, is what matters.

It was March 1942—an important date. But March of the next year was to be even more important for the protagonists of that evening.

# X / THAT MONTH OF JULY

Between April and May, while the Soviet army, for the first time since the German attack, pushed beyond its old borders and penetrated Rumania, Czechoslovakia, and Poland, the war in Africa was over. The alternating series of retreats and advances came to an end on May 12 at Cap Bon in Tunisia, with the surrender of the surviving German and Italian forces. Radio London intensified its signal, and Colonel Stevens, whose voice had become the cherished friend of every listening family, announced: "Italians, your hour draws near!"

Barely two months later, on July 10, Sicily was invaded. The Anglo-Americans established a beachhead on Italian soil, and now the inhabitants did not know whether to rejoice or weep, or rather, more simply, to tremble. It is difficult, after all this time, to reconstruct the exact sequence of events. But the emotional reactions of the population and of individuals cannot even be imagined, unless we were to have the unexpected good fortune to recover some document of the time.

July 19 represented an important date for Rome, which no one thought to commemorate after a lapse of nineteen centuries: the day, in the year A.D. 64, when the colossal fire was started that destroyed the city, and which was supposedly set by the emperor Nero. But July 19, 1943, assumed a different and even more important meaning for the citizens of Rome.

Let us take a look at some notes written shortly afterward by one of Monferini's students:

"On the morning of July 19, 1943, I got up later than usual. The weather promised to be sultry and I had nothing to do. For some time there had been no means of public transportation; it took quite an effort to get across the city. And besides, the Romans themselves no longer seemed so lively and amusing. Their minds were tired, and they no longer found even the strength to exercise their usual talent for satire on propaganda that was proving to be absolutely incapable of understanding, much less controlling the situation. They were calling for something new, grumbling about the food shortages, laughing at the measures taken by the authorities, but they ended up, as they say in good Roman dialect, by 'swallowing it.'

"Rather than face the daily melancholy spectacle of a population that wanted only to sleep and ignore everything and everybody, I decided to shut myself up in my room and go on reading Rousseau's *Confessions*, which I had begun some time ago but had never been able to finish.

"Stifling my yawns, I was plowing ahead with the book when, at about eleven o'clock, the air-raid siren went off. This was distracting, but for some time now it had been happening with a certain frequency. But no Allied aircraft had ever been seen over the city, and this helped to feed the resentment of the Italians against the capital's inhabitants, who were usually thought of as idlers and parasites.

"The door of my room burst open, and I saw the scared face of the woman who came in the morning to do the household chores: 'It's the siren!' I made a nonchalant gesture and went back to my book. But now, almost immediately, explosions could be heard: not so much explosions as a distant, indefinable roar. Little by little one became aware of an uninterrupted boom, which constantly grew in volume. The woman came running back to my room, uttering words I'd never heard before: 'They're bombing Rome!'

"At the same time we heard an unspecifiable number of airplanes passing over our heads, their engines sounding quite unusual, a regular, prolonged droning in a baritone key. Without knowing what we were doing, we rushed down the stairs, to the accompaniment of ever louder explosions, slamming doors, tinkling and shattering windowpanes, strident and hysterical cries.

"Up until the day before, we had gone on repeating the refrain about the inviolablility of Roman skies. Even now it was hard to believe we were really being bombed. We gathered in the cellar, unsure of what to do, but the bravado with which we had greeted other alarms was forgotten. Women despaired for their husbands and children; someone mentioned the dense fumes already rising from nearby neighborhoods that had been hit. And the noise steadily increased, in a crescendo of roars and explosions, while the walls of the house trembled as though in an earthquake. One wave of planes was followed by another. I tried to stay calm, but my extremities were icy cold, and I couldn't keep still. The ceiling of the cellar hung over us like a canopy of lead, making it hard to breathe.

"Finally, after how long I can't say, there was a respite. Silence reigned for a few moments, one heard only a subdued and stifled sobbing, an anguished moaning, from those who were already anticipating the spectacle of devastation that was later to greet our eyes.

"The bombing began again, more violent than before; sometimes it seemed to fade in the distance, other times it sounded as though the planes were dropping their bombs directly over our heads. New moans and new prayers rose from the women; they invoked forgotten names, repeated words of faith, knelt on the floor. Everyone instinctively groped for that pledge of divine protection that the solicitude of mothers imposes on the most unbelieving men: amulets,

medals, rosaries. But already many felt as though they had
always lived in the midst of bombings. Only when a more
violent explosion came, did one see someone abandon himself to despair, then sit down again with a look of stupor on
his face.

"During another pause, we emerged to take stock of what
was happening. The sky, which had been very clear in the
morning, was darkened by a dense haze, rising ominously in
the direction of the Cemetery. The streets were strewn with
shrapnel. Everyone who set out to explore ran back at the
slightest noise. When after three hours of bombing, the all-
clear sounded, we looked at each other in dismay: now we
really had to go and look.

"The neighborhood hardest hit was that of San Lorenzo
fuori le Mura, where, among other things, the basilica of that
name had been destroyed. The avenue running alongside the
Città Universitaria and toward Parioli was thronged with people. Long lines of carts, most of them pulled by hand, tied up
traffic; on top of them were the few household goods that had
been saved, with here and there a scorched mattress, or a
dirty, ragged child, sunk in an awesome silence.

"It was just at the time when the authorities had chosen to
post in the streets instructions to be followed in the event of
an enemy invasion, which only increased the terror.

"Toward evening, a friend and I decided to visit the
bombed area. It was a long walk, since the streets were con-
gested and the trams weren't running. Everywhere the tracks
were torn up, and there were big craters in the ground; our
breathing was hampered by the clouds of dust hanging over
the huge piles of rubble. We regretted having come here to
satisfy our morbid curiosity.

"Squads of soldiers had begun the first rescue operations. Ambulances went by loaded with the wounded, while
in secluded corners out of sight, corpses were piling up,

mercifully covered with whatever rags it was possible to collect.

"Many houses looked intact, but inside everything had collapsed, beginning with the stairs, and it was necessary to go in by the windows. In the days that followed, I was able to observe that often even corpses showed neither wounds nor mutilation. They had remained rigid in the most ordinary positions, immobilized by the concussion of the air. A woman, once pregnant, lay on her back on the floor: her belly had been ripped open and the fetus hurled five or six meters away.

"We then realized that the swarms of fugitives had been the most courageous, those who in some way had reacted to the tremendous shock. Most people sat stunned before the ruins, without moving or speaking, staring at nothing, devoid of even the slightest expression of suffering.

"In a building completely split in two, a large mirror was still hanging, miraculously untouched. From the curious crowd of onlookers, came the voice of a small boy: 'Good thing it didn't break—otherwise it would mean bad luck.' I felt the urge to throw my arms around him and kiss him. In his words, I recognized the rather arrogant courage—which many call cynicism—of the true Romans. I felt certain that despite the disaster, there was still something alive in the city, and a little hope came back to my heart."

The events of this July 19 changed the face of Rome if not the character of its citizens; but they also influenced the state of mind of at least some of Monferini's students. It should be mentioned, however, that in this respect they continued to have many doubts, at least for the time being. Actually there had been too much discussion during all those years. And only now did some at least begin to understand.

This can be see in a letter that reached Rome on July 24, written by one of the few persons who that year had had the privilege—or misfortune, it still wasn't possible to say—of taking a summer holiday.

"Dearest, your letter, received this morning, moved and upset me very much. Not so much for the description of the effects of the bombing on Rome, as for the effect that it seems to have had on your mind. With all the best will in the world toward you, forgive me if I can't completely believe in your sincerity. Of course, it's your own fault, since you've all too often given proof of your superior mind and your contempt for human weakness. Thus it seems to us almost impossible that a bombing, no matter how terrible, could have so radically changed your ideas and your way of thinking. If it's really as it seems from what you say in your letter, it would be a wonderful thing. . . . Meanwhile I can tell you that on this subject a number of factions have formed in our house. My mother and sister (they cried reading your letter) defend your sincerity, my cousin says it's all false and ironical, and I (forgive me, my love) am like Hamlet. From the very beginning I noticed something strange, unusual, and I was moved, then it left me undecided. We too have had a good scare, though of quite another kind, and we've been very apprehensive. For two days we were without news, except for those laconic and by no means reassuring announcements on the radio. It was impossible to telephone or send a telegram, and no visitors or newspapers arrived. We met all the trains in the hope of seeing someone arrive with news, and you can imagine how conflicting and fantastic it all was, always worse than the reality. . . ."

Truth is always relative, and those who judge things with the advantage of hindsight are naturally led to ascribe to facts an importance that corresponds better to reality, and much less to their wishes. And this should be kept in mind in considering an account that has so far remained unpublished, having unexpectedly re-emerged from the dust of a drawer and the dimness of memory.

"On Thursday of that same week, the Fascist Neighborhood Group sent two representatives to our house to ask for clothing and money for victims of the bombing. That afternoon I went to its headquarters, which wasn't far away, taking a big bundle of linen. I confess that in crossing the threshold of the place, I felt a bit intimidated. The strangest stories were told at home about that building. Sometimes, from outside, I had seen rifle racks and contraptions whose purpose was mysterious (actually they were used for parties and dances) and individuals in uniform, with grim, martial faces. I was taken into the office of the secretary of the Fascist Women's organization, where I was received with unexpected cordiality. They showed much appreciation for what I had done, although to avoid misunderstandings I stated that I was a Jew, and they gave me an itemized receipt for the things I'd brought. The room was full of clothes and linens, and I was very glad to have been able to contribute.

"I went out thinking the devil wasn't so bad as he's painted in our imagination. I was almost out of the place when I was stopped by a young fellow in military khakis who demanded in a shrill Fascist voice: 'What year were you born?'

" '1924.'

" 'What do you do?'

" 'I'm a law student.'

" 'Then come with me. You're recruited for Civilian Service.'

"I obeyed, quite annoyed about the whole business, but thinking that as soon as I told them I was a Jew, I'd be spared any further bother. The racial laws were at least good for this, to get out from under the orders of the local bosses—no rallies, no parades, no demonstrations of forced enthusiasm for us.

"The young man had sat down. Behind him, I could see a bronze representation of Mussolini's slogan 'book and gun.'

" 'You know the present situation. Our enemies have started bombing Rome, and unfortunately we don't have the proper organizations for emergency aid. So we've decided to set up a flying squad, made up of willing fellows with guts. We'll give you a uniform and a revolver, and we'll all be there when we're needed.'

" 'I like the idea a lot, and especially the revolver. In fact, I've been thinking of something like that myself. There's one drawback, though: I'm Jewish, and I don't suppose you could accept me.'

" 'Well,' said the young man, and he held out a pack of cigarettes, 'let me tell you something. At this moment our country is in serious danger, and there are no more differences of either race or party. Up until yesterday I was even a Communist, I carried a red flag in my pocket and sang the Internationale. But today, Fascist or not, it's a question of saving Italy.

"How could I object to that? 'I agree, it's a question of humanity, more than politics. I'll tell some of my friends about it too, if you don't mind.'

" 'Good! We're starting right now. My name is Carlo Alberto, and I'll be the squad commander. You'll be my lieutenant, of course.'

"Later, among friends, we discussed whether or not to accept the offer. We decided to do so, because, humanitarian reasons aside, here was an opportunity to enter into contact with Fascist groups and carry out a concrete plan of propaganda and education, something we'd often thought about. And we also had a great wish to re-establish ties with the outside world, from which we'd been separated, but to the point of feeling pride in the separation.

"It was about seven in the evening when we went back to

present ourselves at the Casa del Fascio. In a climate of youthful cordiality, we agreed on orders and assignments. Shortly thereafter we met the local boss, a timid, dried-up little man, whose dream, expressed in long drawn-out sighs, was to avoid any possible trouble. And instead he was faced with a problem of some importance. The owner of a store badly damaged in the air raid had offered the Group almost three tons of potatoes—in wartime the equivalent of a load of gold—and someone had to arrange to collect them. The boss was afraid that this business would delay his supper, and was ready to postpone everything till the next day. Besides, there were no men available. But Commander Carlo Alberto, delighted with the opportunity, came to attention with a resounding click of his heels, and exclaimed: 'Don't worry, sir! I'll find someone to go. I give you my word, by tonight the potatoes will be safe.'

"As the appointed leader of the little expedition, I was given a pass that gave me free access to the bombed area, which was surrounded by cordons of troops. A young volunteer was also put at my command, to act as my guide to the various offices and headquarters. Firmly resolved not to return without our load of tubers, we got on our bikes and set off in the direction of San Lorenzo.

"Unfortunately things did not go as we'd hoped. After much searching, we found the store, but of the potatoes, as they say in adventure stories, there was not a trace. We hunted in the nearby streets but came up with nothing, and the fact that we had been sent by a Fascist Group only increased people's reticence and distrust. Then a painful odyssey began through dirty and disordered offices: the Casa del Fascio, the police station, the carabinieri. No one knew anything about anything, often we were greeted with insults, while everyone did his utmost to make the situation, in itself anything but clear, even more chaotic. We struck up a conversation with a platoon of carabiniere trainees, hurriedly pressed into service, but no one had thought to give them any tools. These boys griped bitterly, and we sympathized with them; they had lost any feeling of respect for their superiors and spoke openly of insubordination and revolt.

"When, dead tired from our exertions, we decided to go back, it was very late at night. We tried to console the little Fascist boss, telling him that maybe the famous potatoes had been taken in by some other Neighborhood Group. His response was disconcerting: 'That's just what I'm afraid of. I know what happens in other Party groups—it's total corruption!' . . .

"The next two days went by rapidly, full of unexpected things. The volume of work was truly overwhelming. It was no use going to San Lorenzo: the stench was such that nothing could be done without a minimum of hygienic precautions, which we, on the other hand, were unable to adopt— we had no equipment whatsoever. There was no water, and it was almost the end of July.

"I was sent to a food rationing office, but not having eaten myself, it only made things harder. People milled around our tables, numbed by the yelling of the soldiers, tormented by insects, brutalized by the heat.

"We decided, on our own, to distribute food directly, without asking anyone's permission or bothering about official forms. One must say that our Carlo Alberto did everything to make himself useful. I was entrusted with a certain sum to be distributed at my discretion, without requiring receipts. I was not the only one to be trusted in this way. But these were exceptional times, and no one, so far as I know, took advantage of it for himself.

"The hours went by in a succession of merciful acts and pitiful scenes. One day I was approached by an old woman, all skin and bones, who was asking for something to cover herself with. I took her to the secretary of the Fascist Women's organization, the one who had treated me so courteously at our first meeting. But the little old lady was a true woman of the people.

"The secretary received us sprawled in a fine leather armchair. She was wearing a brand-new uniform with lots of braid. Standing at attention, I explained the situation to her, although with the old woman right beside me, any explanation was superfluous. The female marshal condescended to give her something that at one time may have been a dress, and she did it with the kind of gesture that in our minds we attribute to Alexander the Great when we read how he distributed provinces in his huge empire to his followers. The old woman timidly tugged my arm, whispering, 'Son, underneath . . . underneath . . . I've got nothing on!'

"I got up my courage and returned to the attack, asking for some article of underclothing. It was not much of a request, and was timidly expressed, but it would have been better not to make it. The marshal jumped to her feet in an outburst of rage, shouting, 'You're never satisfied, are you? Our country is dying, and you come asking me for underdrawers. You deserve a good thrashing, that's what!'

"Sunday, after a twelve-hour shift, we were given a little time off. I went with friends to the Cinema Quirinetta, where a French film was showing. It was a gloomy story, like so many others we'd seen. But it had the singular advantage of taking place in the polar regions. Somehow or other, we had the feeling of being on vacation. When the film was over, we went home, hoping to be in time for the news from Radio London. But around nine-thirty the phone rang. It was the secretary of the Group.

" 'Come down here right away. Wear a black shirt.'

" 'But I just got off duty. And I don't have a black shirt.'

" 'There are important announcements. Shirt or no shirt.'

" 'But I don't have time . . .'

" 'Then go to hell!'

"I hung up, while already from the street I could hear a babble of voices. The radio, the Italian radio, was announcing something that had caught the attention of the Italians. It was reporting that His Majesty the King and Emperor had received the Cavalier Benito Mussolini and accepted his resignation."

As for the invitation delivered over the telephone, it would very soon come true as a result of that announcement, for both sender and recipient, and beyond anything they could have imagined.

## XI / ROME IN DARKNESS
## (WITH BACKGROUND OF FLAMES)

Everything, the true, the likely, and what might have been wished for, has been written about July 25 and the next day, when the Italians realized that Fascism had finally fallen after more than twenty years. The most vivid memory, of little historical or ideological importance to some citizens—and it is one still unknown today, or simply forgotten by professional historians—is of an individual who ran along the Corso shouting: "The Tiber! The Tiber's on fire!" People laughed heartily, without knowing why. A few more thoughtful ones shook their heads, mindful of the incalculable consequences that the fall of the government might bring, including general madness.

But madness, as Shakespeare teaches us, always has an inner logic, and a connection, however slender, with basic reality, and which eludes common sense.

The offices of *Il Tevere* (The Tiber), the Fascist daily, whose editor-in-chief was Telesio Interlandi, were indeed burning. As we were later to realize, the fire, which had scarcely broken out when it was apparently extinguished by four upright volunteers, was destined to take on larger dimensions: all of Italy was on the point of bursting into flame.

But at the time, no one was in a position to foresee this. And even if they had, it wouldn't have bothered them—quite the opposite. Hurrah for the flames, if they carried off twenty years of humiliation and national absurdity! Hurrah also for the fire on the sacred river, if it could sweep away the shame of imperial memories, the prime source of so much provincial megalomania, so many inferiority complexes and accumulations of bureaucratic procedures! And still today in Rome, the problems of urban sanitation cannot be resolved without consulting the Fine Arts Administration, and without some eminent Romanist immediately getting into the fray.

Not to mention besides that a fire on the river might somehow bring to the surface the golden candelabrum of the Temple of Jerusalem, the precious *menorah* that Titus's legionaries had stolen from the people of Israel and their priests. It was for a long time one of the major attractions of Roman tourism, until, as we learn from the *Mirabilia*, it ended up at the bottom of the Tiber during one of the barbarian invasions. And there it still lies, protected from other invasions and the incredulity of people, who are always reluctant to lend faith to poetic legends. And yet Belli, highly expert in things Roman, spoke clearly:

They know it's there, but not even a dog can get at it,
'cause it lies at the bottom of the river.

You want to know just where?
Near the Ponte Rotto, and if they wanted
it could be raised for a crust of bread.

Those who were away from Rome in those days could not even imagine certain things. But they suffered just as much from the separation, which had cut off communication just at the most eagerly awaited moment. On August 10, Marcella wrote from a small town on the Adriatic: "Even now what has happened seems to me a dream. I still wake up in the middle of the night, thinking and wondering if everything that has

happened is true. I've experienced some wonderful and terrible hours. It doesn't seem to me possible. I can imagine
what suspenseful days all of you in Rome have been having.
Too bad we weren't together at this time, since we've spent
so many pleasant and unpleasant hours together and shared
our joys and sorrows with each other. Yet I've been very
happy here, but the atmosphere has been different, and whatever satisfaction everyone may have felt, no one can know
how we've felt. I've thought of you often during these days,
and of all our friends. For five years we've been longing for
this moment, and now, however things may turn out, we'll at
least have the satisfaction of being like everyone else and
being able to look to the future with a certain hope."

One who was particularly missed among those who were
away was everyone's friend Monferini, who had gone to join
his family in Piedmont. One could imagine his satisfaction,
but it would also have been an enormous pleasure to hear
him express it in his own voice. For once he would not have
exercised his critical acumen, nor listened to his inner de-
mon, which was that of contradiction. But on August 16, a
postcard still postmarked with the Fascist slogan *"Vincer-
emo"* (We Shall Win), now so clearly made ridiculous by
events, contained his opinion:

"My dear boy, I've written to a lot of people, but not yet to
you, who by your welcome letter really deserved it. I wasn't
overly enthusiastic at first, but now I'm slowly wiping the
smirk off my face. Nevertheless I'm afraid it will be hard to
avoid the dangers hanging over our country; even the open-
city declaration won't, I think, have any effect.

"Here every night there's pandemonium, and it seems to
me it's all part of a systematic plan.

"You're right to forget about discussions, for the time being all you can do is go along as best you can. I worry quite
a bit about having to leave my family this winter too, since I

don't see any probability that our problems will soon be solved.

"Greetings to all, and warm thanks to all those who have thought of me."

As usual, he was being contrary. But even those in Rome were in the wrong with regard to him: they had told him a big lie. Discussions were still going on, but of a different kind and with different interlocutors. During the brief interregnum of the first Badoglio government, the protagonists of the real struggle against Fascism, survivors of prison and of internal exile on the islands, had begun flocking back to Rome.

Many young people gathered around one of them in a house on the Via Livorno. Eugenio Colorni was a professor of physics and mathematics, but above all an ardent fighter for democracy. The expectations of those longing to meet old-time opponents of the regime, those who had paid in person for their foresight and integrity, was matched on the other side by an understandable curiosity: to be able, after years of forced isolation, to observe some specimens of the younger generation, the fruits that had ripened in the seclusion of the Fascist hothouse.

And there were many, all too many, things to be said. It took infinite patience, on Colorni's part, to listen to the dogmatic rigmarole of those who imagined a prompt and definite solution to all problems, or to correct his interlocutors' many errors and misinterpretations without seeming to, and without offending them.

Someone said: "No matter how things go, the Vatican will have to express an opinion on Italian matters. That's not to say it won't be a vital opinion. In any case, important." These words were the result of the particular experience that had developed in the classrooms of the Istituto Lateranense, where many problems were discussed, and where, especially among young people, many possibilities took shape.

But Eugenio Colorni shook his head, and murmured thoughtfully, showing by his tone of voice how little he was convinced, "The Vatican comes into it, of course. Anyway, we'll see, we'll see."

To the young people, on the other hand, it seemed absurd that in these tumultuous times he should take the trouble to distribute publicly a clandestine little newspaper called *L'unità europea*. Europe? they asked themselves—what's that? Europe contained the Nazi monster Hitler, and almost nothing else. Churchill's England seemed a remote legend. France could be written off for good. What counted above all was Italy, overrun by many clashing armies; and then there were the Italians, meaning everyone, men and women, and including those present. What did Europe signify except a pure abstraction?

Perhaps only the harsh light of recent events could justify the sense of consternation that determined people's judgments and views. There was a whole procession of hitherto unknown problems, an adducing of arguments previously not even suspected. Things began to be called by their right names, and not by cryptic turns of phrase. But democracy, with Marshal Badoglio's government of technicians, was still something less than a modestly proclaimed name. The newspapers—and in particular *Il Popolo di Roma*, edited by Corrado Alvaro, a writer of outstanding civic leanings—came out with large blank spaces in its columns, and especially its editorials. This meant there was still censorship, though it presented itself for what it was. And that already seemed like a lot.

In this blinding and uncertain climate, the feeling came to the fore from time to time of how extremely difficult it would be to find a solution to certain problems. The Allies would inevitably advance from occupied Sicily onto the territory of the peninsula. But when? And how long would it take? Would the chain of the Apennines, the backbone of our country and practically its whole body, allow them to advance rapidly northward toward the large cities? Meanwhile the Germans formed a threatening reality, which every day took on greater proportions. It was enough to look at the railways and the major arteries in Rome: every day witnessed more men, transport vehicles, and weapons, all with the insignia of the Reich, in the heart of Italy.

There were more meetings presided over by Eugenio Colorni, but they were no longer held in the little apartment on the Via Livorno. The group, now expanded, moved to a large salon, decorated in a grand but severe style, on the Via degli Scipioni, in the heart of the Prati quarter. It was a house, or rather a villa, that Monferini's students had never been inside during the five years just passed, although one of their female classmates lived there.

Sylvia Elfer was tiny, with dark hair and a face somewhat too pale, but with a mouth that always wore a very determined expression. She was a conspicuous presence, even though in class she did not join in the uproar and discussions of the others. She always kept her distance, not disdainfully, simply with a certain pride. Even on the tram, the famous Circolare Rossa tram in the morning, she sat apart from the others, unconcerned with comments on the little incidents in school, or the romantic passions that originated there but fortunately developed outside. There could have been, and were, several reasons for her behavior: she came from a family that was not strictly Roman and probably from a higher social level than most of her classmates. Come to think of it, much higher.

But in her beautiful and silent house, which was reached by crossing a marvelous garden, one immediately became aware of another reason for her separation from others. Her brother Eugenio, a little older than she, a good-looking boy with a broad forehead shaded by soft black hair, and who walked with a slight limp, was obviously Sylvia's great true love. His gentle, penetrating eyes, framed by a pair of light glasses, gave the impression of a capacity for understanding and judgment above the average. And immediately after formulating a judgment, those eyes, as though by instinct, sought others, always those of Sylvia. Between brother and sister there was a familiarity, a bond of esteem and mutual understanding that was certainly enough to keep the world, all the rest of the world, a thing apart.

Now with the rush of events, Sylvia and Eugenio broke through the confines of their splendid kingdom and resolved to make contact with the inhabitants of other planets. It was hard to say if it was the approaching storm that drove them forth, or if someone situated on high and therefore unknown to common mortals gave them a new watchword, to emerge from their five-year isolation and place themselves, with due caution, on the same plane as others, whom they were to comfort by their presence. Probably it was simple instinct, the old law of the herd, that led them to re-establish communication at the moment when the woods all around them were beginning to vibrate—one didn't yet know why—from an unspecified danger.

Eugenio Colorni's somewhat professorial voice was growing increasingly grave. What for others was only a suspicion was becoming for him an absolute certainty. The Badoglio government seemed to him not simply wavering on what line to take toward the Anglo-Americans and the Germans, and how to translate it to the plane of concrete action, which was nevertheless imperative. It now seemed to him obvious that the court and the government were in agreement on only one point: to prevent the formation of a solid front of the population, in which anti-Fascists and ordinary citizens, students, workers, and soldiers would find the unity that the moment required and create a bulwark against the enemy. And this was the only thing in which one could put one's hopes.

Eugenio Colorni, of course, did not give up. He mentioned the connections that had been established with the very few factories that existed in Rome, and with the soldiers' barracks. He mentioned the weapons that would come out of those barracks. With weapons available, the dialogue with the Germans would be different.

Certainly he had to be aware of—and Eugenio Elfer noticed it too—the perplexity his words aroused in all those around him. As though at that moment each were saying to himself: So we're in it for good.

"I've spoken to a few officers," said young Elfer. "They said they agreed, they've recognized that there's no other way."

Colorni foresaw another objection. "We'll have to practice, and myself first of all. I've never held a pistol in my hand."

His listeners pondered in their hearts the meaning of this explicit confession. He who had spoken, an authentic and indisputable representative of the opposition to the regime, had fought his battle with only the splendid weapons of his mind: his faith in mankind, his knowledge of mathematics, his books, his unshakable dignity. And he had been the winner: the regime had ignominiously vanished, while the anti-Fascist Colorni was there, ready to resume the old discussion, which besides had never been totally broken off. This was a marvelous confirmation that the path unconsciously taken by Monferini's students, the only one, in any case, that they had been able to see, the path of debate, of constant interrogation of themselves, of history, and of the world, was not wholly mistaken. And perhaps one day it would bear the fruit of other ideas and results. One had to have the strength to wait.

Dealing with the Germans was another matter. Everyone understood that it would be a question of life and death, of simple survival. But in these moments it was precisely this perception that turned out to be paralyzing. Was it possible that a dialogue couldn't be opened even with the Germans, at least with some of them? Was it possible that never, neither now nor later, would one be able to consider them as human beings?

And time was running short. The great consular roads continued to disgorge men, transport, and arms: the sinister wave of swastikas was spreading everywhere. It looked as though that overwhelming war machine could be stopped only by another one, equally efficient and stronger. But where were the Anglo-Americans?

A few hundred kilometers away. Was it possible that their highly perfected technique and overwhelming power were unable to cover that insignificant distance in a single leap? There were two factors on which there could be no doubt: that the Italian government already considered itself beaten, and that the Italians were longing to be freed. Two observations so obvious as to dispel many uncertainties in people's hearts, and cause a minimum of hope, despite everything, to re-emerge.

It was better, much better, not to think about it. The days passed, and nothing changed. After the wonderful and dramatic events of July, history showed no sign of resuming its motion. Everything remained in suspense. And nerves were taut.

Father Arcangelo, one of the recent friends at the Lateranense, wrote on September 2 from the Valdarno:

"I wanted to wait and go to Florence for those books before writing you, but I've decided to do it now because, given the present situation, the course of lectures has been canceled. Who knows when they'll bring it up again! I'm sorry because I had prepared all the material. First I'll go back to Rome.

"Here in the Valdarno, we're enjoying much calm for the moment and eating reasonably well. I'll stay until the beginning of the academic year. But will the University reopen this year? I doubt it.

"How are things going now in Rome? Now that it's an open city, you must be breathing somewhat more easily. Let's hope that God in his mercy grants all of us the possibility of breathing, I don't say easily, but well enough in an atmosphere of peace, order, and brotherhood.

"I'll end this quick note, but promise to write again when I have more time."

There followed a postscript, which showed the writer to be very precise and confident, despite his reasonable pessimism.

"P.S. I'll send the books you so kindly lent me back to you in Rome as soon as I get a chance, since for the moment I have no more use for them."

Let's wait—let's do something. And once again, we'll do something—we'll decide. And so the most absurd interests and expectations were constantly being interwoven and mingled, against the cloudy and uncertain background of hope, which, however, all too often took on the color of uncontrolled fear. The slow banality of everyday life, the stale thoughts that struggled to occupy the endless hours, helped to preserve, from one moment to the next, one's faith that life would come into view at the end.

In those same days, Laura wrote from the Adriatic coast:

"I've fallen right back into an atmosphere of hysteria and madness, having started to read *The Possessed*. I like it well enough for now, but I think it will be the last book by Dostoevsky that I'll read for a while. I want something different, because he's really too insane. Find me something else over which to go wild; I like going wild over some writers, because then I read them more willingly.

"When you speak of the work you have, I hope you'll also

think of me, if I return to Rome, as I hope to do. If the universities really open, I'll enroll, although my father would rather I got married—I'd have to be out of my mind! I'd prefer to study and do something to earn a little money. So since it seems you're moving in such high intellectual and cultural spheres, you should think of me. Otherwise, why did I go on cultivating your friendship for all these years?

"To turn to more serious matters, of which unfortunately there's no lack, here we're going through a lot of uncertainty. It looks as if they're going to send us all away from the coast, but others advise us not to go to Rome just now. Anyway it's almost impossible to travel by train, and it's very hard to find an automobile or truck.

"Every day we hear dozens of conflicting stories, and we don't know whom to believe. Meanwhile 'they' are on the way up! But if Rome, as it seems, is not declared an open city, and 'they' can come back again, we'll think twice about returning, since we've managed to avoid the other bombings. So we keep postponing our departure from one day to the next, but with the fear of suddenly finding ourselves cut off.

"If we don't go back soon, write me often about the situation in Rome and what's being done for us. Certainly it's such a serious moment that our problem is secondary—except, however, that just now there are small signs of a favorable attitude. For now the most important thing of all is to save our skins, then we'll see. When there's peace for everyone, we'll have it too. . . ."

This letter bears the date September 8, 1943. Most likely it was written and mailed in the morning, for in the afternoon came the news of the signing of the armistice. One can suppose that the reading of Dostoevsky was interrupted.

An endless line of Italian tanks began filling the streets of Rome. No one could have imagined that we still had so many forces. It meant that not all was lost, and that the worst, represented by the German forces present in Rome, could be averted. But then it was noticed that the four divisions were moving toward the Via Tiburtina, and turning eastward, where there were neither the Germans nor the Anglo-Americans, who had just landed at Salerno. It was still not known that they had been sent to cover the shameful flight of the king and Badoglio. Hope, however, began to fade.

Eugenio Colorni and Eugenio Elfer were seen in the vicinity of the army barracks, urging the distribution of weapons. Despite their pleas, they got nothing.

At Cecchignola, the last grenadier recruits obeyed one of the very few dignified orders issued that day. Heirs to a splendid tradition, they went to die alone, in silence.

People ventured out toward the Appian Way and the Via Prenestina, eager to see the approach of General Clark's tanks. So many ridiculous rumors were circulating, and this was one of them.

Then night began to fall, a night that was to last nine months, the time needed for the perfection of a human life. Instead, it was a time devoted to death.

A few days later, two more letters from the Adriatic coast somehow got through to Rome. There is a strange effect in rereading them after so many years. Fond feelings, and others that are almost childish. Descriptions of huge and tragic events, and little facts of everyday life. Expressions of wisdom, and naive illusions. Perhaps there is only one thing that can explain and justify it all: the instinct for survival at the age of twenty. The first letter was from Laura.

". . . We're in a state of alarm. It's the first time since the armistice that the sirens have sounded again, and this time we're really scared. There are many Germans encamped around here and others not far away. We can hear a heavy bombardment not far off, perhaps Ancona, but here we don't know what to do, and it's even dangerous to go into the countryside. What's more, since yesterday we've had two earthquake shocks, and they won't be the last, because this area is very subject to earthquakes and once they start they go on for quite a while. Altogether a cheerful prospect, and naturally our morale is very low. I won't tell you how we spent the days following the famous September 8, when I was in a fairly good mood and wrote you the last letter. Here we were calm and there was no danger, but all the news, all the rumors, and the masses of ragged, hungry soldiers passing by have been a rather demoralizing combination.

"The best thing is that here it's still Italy. These villages are definitely paradise on earth; I'll never get tired of praising them. Just imagine, we'd seen Italian, German, and English soldiers and officers, escaped prisoners from the nearby camps, all walking around at the same time undisturbed. Now it's a little different, but there's no real German command. But I think this week we'll go inland for a while, to a little village in the hills where we've taken a couple of rooms. It will be awful, but it's only for a short time.

"I wanted so much to go back to Rome and begin a new life, hopefully of study and work. But after everything that's happened, I don't see anything clearly, and I don't mind staying here a little longer. The company's not bad, and we'll find some way not to die of boredom. The other day I again took a wonderful swim, the last one, I'm afraid, because now it rains a lot. But when the sun is out, the sea is still beautiful. Not to mention all the stars in the sky at night! I've become very sentimental again, but there's a good reason why I don't speak to you about it in a letter, because maybe it wouldn't be understood. I'll only tell you that in the last three weeks I've changed a lot. I mean, maybe I myself haven't changed, but everything that's happened has unsettled me a lot and made me change many of my ideas, and now I see the world and hope for my future in a different way from what I used to think not long ago. In a certain sense, I feel I've aged a little, it's not just that I'm older, more mature, and more full of concrete ideas. All of a sudden I've sort of understood what it is that basically I most want, what it is that can surely make me happy. I can't explain it to you. If you're able to understand what may be the cause of this kind of transformation, which has something to do with the surroundings and especially with the tragic moment we're living in, write and tell me. You can say whatever you like, offend me, scold me. I think you perhaps don't know how dear you are to me. . . . I was so happy when I came to Rome to find friends like you and all the others, much better than any girl friend. They say there's no such thing as friendship between man and woman, and instead we've succeeded in it, and that's really a wonder.* Maybe because every so often we've seasoned it with a pinch of sentimentality and a mutual falling in love.

"I think it won't be long before the bad times start again. Don't leave us without your news, and if any of you are in danger, come here. It's the most beautiful place in the world. . . ."

The other letter was from Marcella.

". . . I think it will be very sad to be away for so long from all the friends with whom we've spent so many hours, because it's now almost certain that we'll spend the winter here. Certainly I have the hope of soon seeing everyone again when things calm down, but now I'm thinking how those years are definitely over, which for us in particular weren't exactly carefree, but still were very beautiful.

"In Rome I grew and acquired a wealth of ideas, which now can be said to form the basis of my personality. Now I'd

---

* To the point that a few years later the letter-writer was joined in matrimony with the addressee, who today is going through these yellowed old papers.

like so much to see all of you again so that you and the others could judge whether I've changed. I've felt very different for some months, kinder, more sensitive than usual, and even rather polite. Maybe all the tragic events that have happened have made me more mature and more serious. On the other hand, I realize how natural certain little-girl attitudes were, as well as the enthusiasms, and all the various plans, and so many foolish things. Now I'm afraid that all this has partly disappeared, and been replaced by a certain correct behavior, greater seriousness and responsibility. Maybe when I'm with my old friends, I'll be able to get back what has been lost. . . ."

What gets lost during the brief journey assigned to each of us is always very difficult to recover. Both these letters are dated October 4, 1943. Less than two weeks later, on the 16th of the same month, more than a thousand Roman Jews were rounded up and deported. And that was only the beginning.

Night, the endless night of German occupation, had definitely fallen. Beyond it, tears, despair, a renewed determination to recover the meaning of what had been lost, and what had never been savored. Nothing and everything. The color of the new day, and whether it would even come, no one could know.

## XII / THE FIRE OVERCOME, THEN EXTINGUISHED

Dawn came nine months later, on June 4, 1944. It was summer, the sun beat down, and the soldiers of the Fifth Army emptied the wine flasks the girls offered them and thought about doing the boogie-woogie. One would have liked to join in their celebration, but there was no time for it. There was a reckoning to be made.

Among members of the old student group, not many were missing. But there was not one who had not suffered some grave loss in his family. Of the whole Jewish Community, which had numbered about ten thousand before the war, more than two thousand had vanished, deported to Germany or Poland. The most knowledgeable and resigned of the survivors soon had the feeling that the others would never return. It was mostly the old people who were gone, having exhorted the younger ones to seek safety—as for themselves, left behind in their homes, what could the Germans do to them? Only in a few cases did the young people stay beside their elders, and they shared their fate. The Nazi madness took them all away, with the pretext that more hands were needed for the war machine. Despite the defeats and difficulties of the moment, it was still able to organize trains of sealed freight cars, criss-crossing almost all of occupied Europe, often for thousands of kilometers. Until they reached the death factories of Auschwitz, Mauthausen, Buchenwald, and Dachau.

Almost all the deportees went to this sorrowful and absurd death. Other Jews perished at the Fosse Ardeatine, in a reprisal carried out by the Germans. Among them was Alberto Di Nepi, one of the most expert antique dealers in Rome, who had kindly and generously lent his house for the students' "revue." But a few individuals from the group, or in some way connected with it, had the privilege—or let us say simply the fate—of dying differently.

During those days, we learned what had happened to Eugenio and Sylvia Elfer. Eugenio, leaving behind the comforts of home and his discussions of utilitarian Zionism, dear to his heart and which was only concerned with the happiness of the Jews, had gone to the Abruzzi Apennines, where he organized the rescue and escape of Allied prisoners of war. Now he had found an unforeseen happiness, and a new reason for living. To his sister, Sylvia, he wrote: "Come, your family is waiting for you," meaning by family those sought by the SS. To his father, however, his message was: "You'll surely forgive me for being more of a good Italian than a good son. Perhaps my life will serve to save many others." And so it was. Eugenio disappeared during one of the numerous trips he made through the lines to take the fugitives under his protection to safety. He disappeared mysteriously, amid the glare of fire at Anzio. But his sister, who had been one of the student group, died soon afterward, shot, through a tragic error, by an American sentry who was obeying orders. Sylvia Elfer, having just crossed the threshold to freedom, expired in the arms of an American doctor, while a Jewish army chaplain murmured to her the ritual words: "Magnified and sanctified be His great name."

Eugenio Colorni, whom some members of the group had met only in the final days, pursued throughout the German occupation his vocation of an underground fighter who did not know how to fire a gun. He died at the end of May, a few hours before the Liberation, shot down on the Via Nomentana by a Fascist death squad.

Claudio Fiorentino, who in his own way belonged to the group, chiefly by courting the girls—and he was a handsome boy, with sparkling eyes and a ready wit—left quietly for Bari as soon as the Allies arrived. Only a few knew his secret: he was afraid it was too late to take part in the fighting. On the farthest edge of southern Italy he underwent rapid training in parachuting and sabotage, and had the privilege of embarking on a plane as one of the first Italians to be treated by the Anglo-Americans as a cobelligerent, almost an ally. The plane crashed in the Umbrian mountains, and thus Claudio, at the age of eighteen, was sacrificed, fighting, but without taking any other human life, as his idealism demanded.

Death was becoming something familiar to these young people. The group tried to reconstitute itself, but it was simply not possible. The underlying conditions had changed, and Monferini was far away in northern Italy, separated by his family situation and the fortunes of war.

But new friends appeared. Among the liberators, there were even men who wore a particular sign on their uniforms—the Star of David. They were soldiers in the Palestine "Jewish Brigade"—Gershon Achituv, Chaim Zilber, Duvdevani, the twins Joseph and Zevi Sternlicht, Zevi Ankori with his moving songs, and many others, young and old, all volunteers who had come to offer their contribution to the common struggle, as well as to gather up the few survivors of the Jewish tragedy. How could one not see them as brothers? People approached them because they were distributing white bread and speaking Hebrew: theirs was the language of Hillel and Shammai, and the only one they used, even in ordinary conversation. And they even embodied Hillel and Shammai. Eliezer Halevy, who in his long career had taken part in many revolutions, a friend of Ehrenburg, and who had reached Paris after a dramatic escape from Siberia, was a man who had studied higher mathematics and allowed no deviations from his ideological rigor. But Izchak Den Dor, a mild Lithuanian Jew with reddish hair and deep blue eyes, had a different notion of conversation and democracy. The phrase that constantly recurred on his lips was *"be-vakasha, la-sheveth*—please, let's sit down"—and he would begin the discussion again, but in a more peaceful form that hushed the tumult. But you soon realized that a peaceful discussion by no means meant giving up the boldest, even wildest ideas. It was Ben Dor himself, cultivator of the Hebrew language and sergeant in the British Eighth Army, who launched one of the most splendid and incredible projects undertaken at that time: the publication of an Italian-Hebrew and Hebrew-Italian dictionary. It was truly a crazy plan, international in scope: Jewish Palestine contributed the idea and the organization; a Hungarian refugee, Nicola Erdelyi, who spoke no less than eighty languages, shut himself up at home to edit the dictionary; while the paper, then completely unavailable, could only have been a gracious albeit unknowing gift from the well-supplied warehouses of His Britannic Majesty, King George VI. Ben Dor thus fulfilled his wish to give to Italy, in particular Jewish Italy, a valuable tool of understanding, with a view to future relations. He returned to his own country in time to die, the victim of a Jordanian bomb during the 1948 siege of Jerusalem.

The discussions continued in a totally new tone. Among the participants was Giorgio, both of whose parents had been taken away during the German occupation. He seemed changed, almost consumed by an inner fire: unlike most, he no longer had any doubts about the path to choose. Or, if he did, they were not apparent.

In his hours and days of isolation he had loosened the grip of worry and fear by drawing up a long manifesto, addressed to "Jews all over the world and of all persuasions, learned Polish rabbis immersed in the study and practice of the Talmud, young Jews in Palestine tempered by hard labor in the fields and the rigorous studies of Mount Scopus, young Russian Jews who have probably replaced the Star of David with the hammer and sickle, American Reform Jews seeking to reconcile skyscrapers and the God of Sinai, and even the rich Jews of London and Paris for whom being a Jew means going to the Synagogue once a year and who still believe in the myth of assimilation, and to baptized Jews who have found in their new faith, sincerely or not, the solution to the problem, and to the young people of all nationalities and all tendencies, you who feel the problem more keenly than others because the crisis has caught you with your minds still virgin and open to everything"—it was to all of them that Giorgio spoke in the hope that they would join him in seeking a solution based on the premises of history.

Unfortunately, the harsh reality of the war prevented him from making more than six or seven copies of his manifesto. Otherwise he might have been heard.

The coming of the Liberation, and the support of his engineer brother, now allowed him to rethink his ideas and to publish a small volume summing up his opinions and choices. Taking his cue from a famous pamphlet by the philosopher Benedetto Croce, he entitled it *Perchè non possiamo non essere sionisti* (Why We Can Only Be Zionists); in it he retraced the spiritual journey of all those years, repeating on the last page the invocation of the fathers: "May he who grants peace in heaven grant peace to us too and to all the people of Israel—amen."

His closest friend, who fully knew his stubbornness, which consisted in a rigorous and implacable consistency of ideas, wrote him in a letter used as a preface: "The task you are taking on today is a sacred one, which will perhaps absorb all your energies and cost you dear; but now there is no turning back."

The group made every effort to evade this harsh truth, even going so far as to stage a second musical revue. Things were much easier this time; locations, musicians, and even money were now available. Once again Gino erupted in his parodies of classical opera, and Giacometta sang in her beautiful voice with its romantic overtones. But it was no longer the same show.

From 1946 to '47, many left. By now definitely detached from the fine odor of respectability and comfort of their bourgeois homes—but the fault was neither the fathers' nor the sons'—they were setting out to be pioneers in Eretz Israel, as the Zionists called it, as part of the still semiclandestine emigration of those years. Giovannino left, as did Laura, Sara, and Marcella. So did Silvio Calò, who had kept to himself in the group, nourishing literary ambitions that might have borne fruit, and he was soon to express the best of himself: he died, gun in hand, defending his kibbutz against the Egyptian invaders in 1948. Giorgio too left, of course, having just married Giovannino's sister Letizia. At the moment of departure he had a violent quarrel with his best friend, but this was his way, more than anything else, of expressing the sorrow he felt at their separation. Monferini, who had just returned from the north, listened frowning, himself in the grip of sorrow.

These pioneers had different experiences in the rediscovered land of their ancestors, but in general they were among the best elements transplanted in the postwar period; not for nothing did they go by their own free choice, and after an invigorating spiritual struggle. But in the beginning it was very hard, and in any case the encounter with a reality that they had only dreamed of was unsettling. Evidence of this can be seen in a letter from Marcella, who from an ideological standpoint was perhaps the least prepared. The letter was written on December 10, 1946, from Neva Hillel—she underlined the name.

"The first impression you get from Eretz Israel is that it's a wonderful place with an endlessly varied landscape, where everything seems to call for silence, peace, and work. Nowhere else do you realize how truly all men want nothing but to work and quietly enjoy the pleasures of family life. And here is where the struggle is, while very many if not all still mourn the loss of their dear ones. Terror and anxiety can still be seen on their faces, but not on those of the children. The children of Eretz Israel are beautiful; they must not suffer, and this may be the reason why they are given such importance and attention.

"I've now begun to know a few people. In Jerusalem I was irritated by the religious fanaticism of some, luckily they aren't many.

"In this place, where I've come for a rest, there's a better atmosphere, many people from the kibbutzim, and in general with progressive ideas. Of course, there's a reason, because it's only open to members of the *Histadderuth*, the trade union confederation. The boys and girls of the kibbutzim are definitely better than the others. You notice in them a kindness and a concern for everyone that is seldom found in individuals who don't live collectively. I haven't spent much time in a kibbutz, and have been able to observe only with the eyes of a guest. At Oghen I particularly liked the circle composed of Czechs, a few Hungarians, and the little group of Italians. It's a small kibbutz, and that's why it has seemed to me more united and harmonious, while Ghivath Brenner I didn't like at all. As a kibbutz it's very well organized, but it's too big, and in the huge dining hall, where so many people gather, I really felt uncomfortable. It's not just the difficulty of living with so many people, and there are other difficulties in the kibbutz, but this is certainly one of the main ones. . . .

"City life in Eretz Israel is no different from anywhere else, except that here everything is simpler, you live in the midst of people who come from all parts of the world, and you're free to behave as you choose. In these last days, when I've been living completely alone in this new environment, I'm become more convinced of many things that before left me rather doubtful. Here I've had a strong feeling of solidarity with all these people. Here there are Russians, Poles, Germans, Rumanians, Sabras,* and myself, the only Italian. Here all languages are spoken, as well as Hebrew, and here there's a whole variety of types who have nothing in common except the fact of being Jews. And yet I now feel that this is the place for me, and that even though there are many things I don't like and which leave me dissatisfied, there's nevertheless a kind of thread that keeps me tied to the destiny of everybody here, and it's impossible to escape it.

"Still I miss my family and dearest friends terribly.

"That's all I'm lacking here, for the rest I'm young and willing, and life isn't easy anywhere. But the separation is terrible, and I don't think it can ever heal.

"Something else about me. I'm beginning to be much more practical and less of a dreamer, I adore music, and here everybody knows how to play an instrument, and they love it. . . ."

Giorgio, too, had started writing letters again from time to time. On his arrival, he had written to apologize for his brusque farewell, and to reiterate his insistence on the need to make a choice: Jewish or not, revolutionary or bourgeois, the important thing was to decide. Then he had plunged into

---

* Young people born in the country, and likened to the fruit of the prickly pear: spiny on the outside and sweet within.

the great fishery in the Beth-Shean valley along the Jordan, and his life took on a completely different character. Discussions about Hillel and Shammai were replaced by the assiduous practice of the more than six hundred rules that rabbinical wisdom has prescribed for man's behavior; by the problem of creating the best possible conditions for breeding millions of carp; and by questions of how to organize a middle-sized kibbutz like his, very complex questions and virtually endless: from large fundamental problems, such as how far to go in abolishing private property, house and money, to such minor sources of disagreement as to whom to assign the more undesirable tasks, how to vary the diet of so many people with such different tastes, how to persuade two individuals who dislike each other to live together in harmony. And also—the most serious problem of all for one-hundred-percent pacifists—how to handle firearms.

From then on he wrote only on special occasions. He wrote when the state of Israel was proclaimed, which had been the goal dreamed by everyone, although everyone doubted that it would ever happen. Rather than joy, he expressed his worries for the future. Would this state survive the clash with its attackers? And the infinitely graver danger of becoming a state like any other? This was not the ancient pride of the Chosen People, but an awareness that only a great effort by man at understanding his own history could allow him to find—who knew when and how?—a way to get along with his neighbors. And meanwhile even Giorgio, a staunch supporter of the need for friendship with the Arabs, was forced to do long stretches of sentry duty, hoping never to have to fire a shot and take another's life.

He wrote again on the occasion of Gino's death, mingling his grief with that of his distant friends. Gino died in the same year that Israel was born, stricken suddenly during a trip to Turin, the first vacation he had allowed himself after the harsh war and postwar years; he died having just passed the age of thirty, and with him went a patrimony of dedicated studies, fertile inspiration, an immense love for his family, his friends, and mankind, and much, much joy.

His friends, as they took leave of him at a ceremony during which some of his finest music was played, tried their utmost, despite their tears, to convince themselves that his was not the most absurd and bitter fate.

"This is not and should not be a sad evening," they insisted. "This is not intended as a memorial service. It is a concert of music written by a young composer, who knew that he deserved the attention and indulgence of others. As such it should be heard, without dwelling on the cruel fate that has suddenly and prematurely cut short Gino Modigliani's thriving life. If anything, the fact that this evening we are able to hear his voice, his artist's voice, and therefore the truest, is reason for consolation, for inner joy. When a man dies, what survives of him is only that portion of affections and emotions that he has been able to communicate to the more or less restricted circle of his family and friends. When an artist dies, a much wider circle of individuals, men and women, are lifted in a powerful wave of sympathy, in a common experience of those feelings and emotions that the artist has expressed in a more universal, more accessible language than the ordinary, namely poetry or music. And if it is true, as it is, that the deepest, most intimate joy is the kind that emerges from feeling oneself united to another person, or to a more or less broad group of individuals, then you must agree with us that this is not and cannot be a sad evening, this November evening, where for an hour or two we can feel ourselves linked together, as known and unknown friends, in the blessed name and memory of Gino Modigliani.

"We who took the initiative in organizing this ceremony, and who were his friends in happy, carefree hours, must confess that we set about carrying out our project as one sets out to perform a painful duty, a duty one would rather not perform. We were thinking the same thoughts that, in all probability, crossed the minds of many of you: let us remember a friend whom we loved very much, through the realization of a dream that he could not very often realize himself, the public performance of his works; let us pay homage to these fruits of a youthful talent before time cancels them in the minds of most.

"But we must also say that the passage of days, perhaps also the excitement that derived from feeling a construction take shape hour by hour that we had feared was too fragile, this growing agreement, this moving outpouring of participation and generous contributions—may God grant that all of us succeed in drawing so much affection to our persons as the good, kind soul of Gino Modigliani was able to arouse!—this unforeseen sequence of emotions, have led us to consider this evening's event in a wholly different light.

"In the course of his brief pilgrimage on this earth, Gino Modigliani wanted and was able to say a word that, until now we can say, has been stronger than his own destiny. This word expresses faith and hope. It is meant to be heard by you with a warm readiness of mind, with your thoughts turned toward a man who, with steady mind and firm will, once again traveled, certainly not for the last time in mankind's history, the eternal paths of music."

These were absolutely sincere words and hopes. As was the conviction that time would dim the memory of such nobly inspired pieces as *Psalm 74*, the *Little Suite*, the *Meditations on the Stigmata of Saint Catherine of Siena*, and many others. Perhaps what would echo the longest of all in people's hearts were the notes written to a mysterious and elusive song by Heine, included in a memorable musical revue:

Auf Flügen des Gesanges,
Herzliebchen, trag ich dich fort,
Fort nach den Fluren des Ganges,
Dort weiss ich den schönsten Ort.

Dort liegt ein rotblühender Garten,
Im stillen Mondenschein;
Die Lotosblumen erwarten
Ihr trautes Schwesterlein.

Die Veilchen kichern und kosen,
Und schaun nach den Sternen empor;
Heimlich erzählen die Rosen
Sich duftende Märchen ins Ohr.

Es hüpfen herbei und lauschen
Die frommen, klugen, Gazell'n
Und in der Ferne rauschen
Des Heiligen Stromes Well'n.

Dort wollen wir niedersinken
Unter dem Palmenbaum,
Und Liebe und Ruhe trinken
Und traümen seligen Traum.

This song represented a hope, and nothing more, for those who had survived so many incredible events, including the fire on the Tiber. Each of them felt as though he were the servant of Job or Melville's Ishmael, of having survived with this single purpose, to be able to report sooner or later what he had seen. And he repeated to himself, in a tone of envy, or else of sorrowful consolation, the classical words of pessimism that run from Menander to Leopardi: those dear to the gods die young.

Meanwhile time was passing. New characters were appearing in the limelight, and new problems were being raised. The Tiber was no longer afire. Its surface, the flames now spent, had gone back to being what it always was, yellow or sickly green, depending on the sun's reflections and the time of day. Who knew how much time would go by before it caught fire again. And yet this must happen, as the age-old history of the city warns us. And once again the flames will have to be put out.

From the streets and squares, which had returned to living almost the same life as before, rose cries that sounded like songs. "America, loose or in packs!" shouted the black-market cigarette sellers. "We're off!" threatened the truck drivers. Or, "It's raining!"—the words that announced an impending police raid.

These were new expressions, and they were added to those that emerged, still alive in neighborhood street stalls, from events and time. "Abruzzo, Abruzzo!" sang the lamb butcher, while the fishmonger, in the tones of a Michelangelo, addressed this dramatic apostrophe to his wares: "Speak up, fish, speak up!" An ageless little old woman, selling herbs, repeated her everlasting refrain, which was not a *memento mori* but a reminder of the banality of life: "Don't forget mint . . ." There were other cries, still heard but soon to disappear: "Umbrella man! Any old umbrellas or basins to be fixed?" Nowadays anyone with an old umbrella or a cracked basin doesn't bother to repair them; he throws them away, as required by the consumer society. And other cries have disappeared forever, surviving only in the verses of Roman dialect poets: "Melons! Who wants them!" "Rags, scrap iron, nails, old shoes!" "Sardines for roasting!" Thus sang our fathers and grandfathers on the streets of Rome, and among them, as Belli tells us, there were also Jews.

Now songs were sung in a different way. In a theater that had just reopened, emerged the pale and tortured mask of Anna Magnani, still bearing the imprint of the terrors suffered while Rome was a city open to every danger and chance. Even

her voice, so passionate and dramatic, had regained its sweetness, as sweet as the song she was singing:

> How lovely, Rome, you are,
> how lovely in the early evening,
> girdled by the Tiber. . .

## XIII / LIFE WITH A CODA

The story of the Tiber afire is irrevocably finished, and there can be no thought of starting over. Anyway who would want to? There is perhaps a very slight temptation to follow up the threads still dangling from the old fabric, the slender traces that lead forward in time and space. But, more than anything, it would be almost impossible. According to the ancients, it was the task of Atropos, one of the three Fates, to cut the threads, the threads of life. And it's the only way we know to conclude, for good but not forever, the histories of men.

The recent death of Martin Buber makes it possible to attempt one of these albeit provisory conclusions. Here is another unpublished paper that belongs in this memoir. It goes back to 1960.

### Meeting with Martin Buber

To be in Jerusalem meant a great many things to me, from a historical, political, and in a certain respect sentimental standpoint. It especially meant the possibility of having a conversation with Martin Buber.

Frankly speaking, I must say I felt that I had known everything about Buber, both as a person and his work, from way back: the dim days immediately preceding the war, when with the first reactions to Fascism and the unexpected revelations of a democratic world and a European culture, I stumbled by chance, in a certain dusty cubbyhole, on one of his youthful works, *Sette discorsi sull'ebraismo*. It is a collection of essays from before the First World War, but which, to someone like myself, who had only realized he was a Jew when the racial laws were promulgated, revealed the foundations and meaning of a Judaism that was not simply a passive and amorphous heritage of tradition. More than anything else, of course, reading this book represented a beginning. But later I returned to it with increasing frequency, as to the one that indicated to me an extraordinarily rich and vital Judaism, fully in keeping with the other sources of my intellectual upbringing: a Judaism seen through the continuity of the centuries as a predominantly religious experience, but in constant conflict with liturgical and clerical crystallizations, and perpetually renewing itself until our own days, while its most profitable and glorious moment remained steadfast, that intoxicating flowering known as prophetism. A Judaism all spirituality and elevation, but made to the measure of man, which fought with varied success the ever recurring involutions of Talmudism, and which appoints man, in the words of Buber and Jewish legend, as "God's companion in the work of creation."

There would be no point in my trying to repeat the discussions that for months and years I and some of my contemporaries devoted to delving into Buber's thought—all the more since our arguments shifted easily to the more scorching plane of political action, in particular the Zionist solution to the Jewish problem.

I must say, however, that even on this plane, it seemed to me that Buber fully answered our needs and wishes: by rejecting the immediate political uses of Zionism—namely, the Zionism that would make Israel "a people like any other," and which washes its hands of its spiritual vocation—and likewise by demolishing, with vigorous irony, the vague, nineteenth-century liberal and deistic utopianism of those who foresaw a formal solution of the Jewish question under the guise of an alleged mission among the nations. For Buber, Zionism was also to be inserted in the golden lode of Jewish history, to which not only Moses and Isaiah, but also Spinoza and Marx, belong: an instrument, to be sure, for redemption from present miseries, but also, and primarily, an exercise in inner renewal, an invitation to the personal and totally purifying fulfillment of individuals and the people—an explicit summons to the pioneer spirit, that pioneer spirit that so many young people were to carry from European universities to the collective settlements of Palestine. And at this point the discussion shifted to the theme of a socialism freed of contingent doctrinaire fetters, likewise to be projected onto the plane of an uplifting inner experience of renewal, this time, indeed, for the benefit of all mankind.

All of this has to do with the days when a very small group of young Roman Jews, cut off from the world, were doing their best to establish some sort of contact with life and reality. Until the day of liberation came, and the group could realize some of the dreams it had cherished, including that of knowing something more precise about the man who had been one of our most valid teachers during the desperate years.

And at this point came disappointment. The soldiers of the Jewish Brigade, to whom we addressed our questions, answered us with grudging and evasive hints. Oh yes, Buber, a great philosopher who taught at the University of Jerusalem, but who by now was completely detached from the pressing problems of the Jewish condition and the reality of the country. A figure worthy of veneration, in memory of the way his words had been able to move the hearts of many young Jewish intellectuals in Germany, who had now turned into farmers—all of them young people, they hastened to add, who had by now taken completely different paths, some returning to the ranks of traditional orthodoxy, others going on to a strictly Marxist brand of socialism. In the remarks of our informants, Martin Buber appeared as a great and learned professor, very old and very isolated, without any steady following in the country. And there was also something else to which these friends, lowering their voices, alluded, a few small sins that not everyone was willing to pardon: his tireless political activity in support of Arab-Jewish friendship, manifested primarily by his demand for a binational state. The disorders that had begun in 1936 had been somewhat lulled by the great war, but the harsh tension in people's minds was still there: to speak of peace with the Arabs after what had happened, and with what was thought to lie ahead, had come, in short, to be judged an unwise act, if not a true failure in one's duty to national solidarity.

Thus my eagerness to widen my knowledge of Buber was frustrated, nor was it later satisfied by reading his more recent works; on the contrary, it was whetted by the attention his fame attracted outside Jewish circles as well, his name being repeatedly mentioned as a candidate for the Nobel Prize; indeed, my admiration for the man not only remained intact, but grew from what I had learned of the inflexibility of his character.

So here I am, twenty years after my first encounter with Martin Buber, seeking an interview with him in Jerusalem. This time everything turns out to be easy, I'm a guest of the Israeli government, and Buber is one of the more conspicuous personalities in the cultural life of the country. At the age of eighty-two, and now retired from teaching, he nevertheless represents a luminous beacon toward which many Europeans and Americans are drawn. My courteous Israeli hosts go out of their way to get me an appointment, committing, however, a small gaffe: they neglect to specify the real reasons for my request and emphasize instead my work in journalism and television. Buber's reply is thus quite firm: he will be glad to receive me, but with the assurance that I'm not bringing a camera, much less any recording equipment.

His house is on a street named after the Choveve Zion, the romantic Lovers of Zion, precursors of political Zionism. It is an attractive shady street in the new part of Jerusalem, ascending steeply to the so-called German Colony. I arrive early in the morning, and am asked to wait a few minutes by a beautiful girl with soft, expressive Yemenite features. The delay gives me a chance to examine the room, in which there is a curious mixture of heavy furniture, undoubtedly Central European in origin, and decorative copper objects, intricately decorated in Oriental style.

After a few minutes I'm taken into Buber's study. Books everywhere, and a small desk next to the window, it too incredibly loaded with books; from behind it emerges a large head, surrounded by an uninterrupted white halo, the hair and beard. A pair of small eyes, gray and penetrating, constitutes the whole life of that face, whose strongly marked features seem molded by the hand of a vigorous and gifted sculptor. The head of a prophet, just as I had imagined it.

I begin timidly, denying that my presence is due to simple professional curiosity, and citing sentimental reasons instead, the still vivid memory of all the good I had derived from his books. I speak Italian, aware of Buber's knowledge of our language, but still I'm surprised when he answers in a clear, correct Italian, albeit separating his words and pronouncing them with a strong German accent. This puts me at my ease and relieves my anxieties.

"I suppose you mean my old books, which were translated into Italian by my dear friend Dante Lattes."

He smiles, with a strange, imperceptible chuckle, which I would say is directed primarily at himself—a smile full of human irony, which was to reappear frequently in our conversation.

"Those are old things, very old, now completely outdated."

I hasten to say that for me they have an entirely personal value, and that anyway, in my opinion, the basis for the positions taken in them is still fully valid today.

"A lot of time has gone by," he replies, "and today the conditions of countries, and those of world Zionism, have changed radically. Fifty, even thirty years ago, Zionism was a small movement of idealists and young people. It did not have great political importance, but was a forum for lively and bitter debate, which was sometimes said to be too rhetorical. Today we have a state, and it's a reality, indeed a splendid reality, and I say so without irony. It has welcomed Jews of every kind and from every place: the great Eastern emigration—Yemenites, Persians, Moroccans, Libyans, Tunisians—has given our nation a new look, and no one today would dare to predict what its final appearance will be. And even the prospects have changed. The political ruling class is still today the one that built the state, but the force of events has led it to correct many ideas, and also many goals. And there's no doubt that in the long run the country will end up with the expression of a majority different from the present one, in which the new forces that compose the nation will be reflected."

"That's the inevitable order of things. But does it seem to you that the new situation represents a retreat in the spiritual condition of the Jews?"

"What has happened before our eyes is, in any case, a marvelous thing, exceeding the expectations of our boldest dreamers. As for the inevitability of historical processes, it's true that men are required to adapt themselves to it, but we shouldn't forget that we're given the possibility of modifying and correcting, at least in part, anything that goes against our aspirations. And this too should be said: not everything is as fine and satisfactory as it may appear from the outside; indeed we should be surprised if it were."

"What do you mean specifically?"

"One of the outstanding defects that I notice in the present situation is its excessive politicization. By this I don't mean the splitting up of political forces—that's another matter, of a technical kind, I'd say. I'm speaking of an ever growing tendency that seeks to reduce at all costs every problem to the single and often deceptive aspect of political expediency."

"Isn't that a typical failing of the whole contemporary world?"

"Of course. It's one of the myths of our time, and ought to be resisted. There's another one, no less dangerous, and that's the one of science and technical progress. What we're called upon to witness are amazing achievements, no doubt about it. But they also contain a grave danger. They make it easier for us to forget one of the fundamental truths underlying our existence: that the spirit moves at a much different pace from that of history. That's why we often find it hard to keep up with many developments that we ourselves have brought about. I don't know when it will happen, but personally I'm sure that the moment will come when contemporary man, in looking at himself and the world around him, will be afraid and feel himself lost. That day will open up new perspectives, no longer in the field of technical achievement, but in that of the spirit."

"Do you see any sign that that moment is approaching?"

"Yes, fortunately for us, and it's restlessness. I'm judging, of course, from the position in which I find myself, almost completely cut off from contacts with the world. But in the young people who seek out my company—not many, but their number is increasing, and they're diligent and in agreement—I feel the ripening of this restlessness, this impatience. The doubt is there, and it's spreading—fortunately for us."

"It remains to be seen whether this return to spiritual values will occur in time to avoid new catastrophes, and in any case, whether we'll be there to see it."

"No one can say what tomorrow will bring. But there's no need to despair. Above all, one has to have patience. For me, it's difficult, at the point I've reached; for you, however, it's different. You can wait, and you'll also be able to see."

Again the twinkling, mysterious smile, as though to remind himself that he has learned to distrust "ultimate solutions." The conversation, which has lasted more than an hour, partly due to the slowness with which Buber speaks, is over. My host gets up, and I am amazed at how small, incredibly small, is the body that supports that majestic head. . . .

The preceding pages were written down more as personal notes for the writer than as a story to be submitted to some newspaper. That they have been held back until today is explained by their scant importance in evaluating the work and moral stature of this singular figure, both of which can be better verified elsewhere; indeed, their most transparent meaning derives from small and very special events, the ones that have been described.

As for the state that Buber yearned for, and the attitude of its younger citizens, the whole world followed with bated breath the course of the Six Day War and its consequences. Not everything is clear for one judging from a distance, often with little knowledge of what led up to it, who considers superhuman the determination with which the Israeli people defended its survival during those days, and who remains doubtful in the face of the debate over future relations with the Arabs and the fate of the occupied territories.

But an answer, albeit a private and indirect one, can be

found in a letter written by Giorgio, from his kibbutz of Sedeh Eliyahu, on June 26 after the war.

After describing the anxiety and heroism of those hours, he concluded as follows: "Let me end with an episode of an almost personal kind. Hearing a younger child speak of *arabushim* (a rather derogatory epithet for our neighbors, meaning 'little Arabs,' like saying *ebreucci* [little Jews] in Italian), my eldest daughter, who had shared with the rest of us the anxieties, the tension, the exertions, the armed vigils, jumped to her feet and said, 'I don't want to hear you talking like that, the Arabs are people just like us.' Hearing this, I thought that we are truly in the right if, even under such conditions, we have succeeded in educating our children to the most elementary human values."

Another disconcerting ending that left unanswered questions relates to the recent death of Professor Lucaroni.

He was not especially ill, but he was old, very old; as it is said of Job, and as one would wish it to be for all just men, he had reached the point of feeling satiated with life. And besides, had not another just man among the just, the janitor Romeo Bondi, ended his days having regained peace and tranquillity, and surrounded by his children?

For some time, Professor Lucaroni had no longer been able to go to the University, where he was faithfully awaited by a new generation of students who, if only to hear his original perceptions, were ready to put up with his incomprehensible Marches accent. As for himself, he continued to pay no heed to the stupidities that go by the name of money, insurance, pension: leaden weights that prevent a man from enjoying the supreme good, freedom. But his friends, petty-minded and much less free, worried about him.

It was Monferini, raising his ever uneasy gaze from his judgment, hesitant but not unfavorable, of Mao's revolution—

"It's not a conviction based on logic, it's an act of faith"—who rallied friends on Lucaroni's behalf.

There were no letters or appeals in the newspapers—at the most a few telephone calls. But from every part of Italy, and from foreign countries as well, contributions and messages overflowing with love poured in. From the Quirinale palace, the official residence of the president of the Republic, someone recalled having found shelter one night during the German occupation in Lucaroni's home. Another wrote: "We were both from the Marches and I met him in the courtyard of a prison: just think, what a coincidence!" And Giorgio, too, at his kibbutz, took up his pen.

"Dear Professor Lucaroni: A kind friend has reminded me that this year marks the twenty-fifth anniversary of the beginning of those Fribourg courses that for two years had a by no means insignificant importance for us young Roman Jews who were anxious in some way to continue our studies. Not always does the celebration of anniversaries and the marking of more or less historical dates correspond to a felt inner need in those who celebrate them, and it's easy to lapse into empty rhetoric. Yet in this case I feel the duty to express to you, as to all those, living and dead, who did so much for the success of those courses, the feelings of gratitude and that have remained intact even after so many years. And I hope it will not seem strange to you that someone like myself, who for various objective and subjective reasons has not continued in the study and application of those disciplines, finds it proper now to recall that episode.

"Indeed, those courses were for all of us not only a happy solution to problems that an absurd ideology and absurd laws had created for us, not only did they furnish an important contribution to our cultural development, but they were also a human experience of prime importance. The dedication and seriousness of the studies, in the teachers as well as in the students, the bond of solidarity and mutual esteem that was created, helped to establish an especially agreeable atmosphere. And perhaps, for us, the greatest source of respect and admiration was the personal example offered by those teachers who, like yourself, came forward to educate and instruct us, moved by a feeling of human solidarity, at a time when to demonstrate solidarity and friendship toward the rejected could be a source of difficulty, and have unpleasant consequences. And again you, perhaps more than all your other colleagues, were a living lesson and palpable example of what anti-Fascism, consistent in itself and profoundly lived in every act of one's life, could and should be. And this was certainly then, in those calamitous times, the highest and most necessary lesson we could receive; and for this reason, I repeat, it was a truly positive human experience.

"The tragic events of late 1943 dispersed those courses, and dispersed us too; each went his own way. I, perhaps more than others, abandoned the premises of those studies and found my way in other experiences of life and other interests. We spoke of this—remember, Professor?—the last time we met, twelve years ago. Then during my last visit to Rome, I gave a talk on my experience of an Israeli kibbutz, and you were good enough to come and hear me. You showed then a great interest in our life, and with all the sincere warmth of your anarchist passion, you gave an interpretation of it that left me impressed, and which, I confess, I have used many times to clarify to myself and others the foundations of our collectivism.

"I therefore take the opportunity of this jubilee to send you my best wishes for your serenity, along with feelings of gratitude and memories that, I repeat, have remained unchanged through the years."

The promoters could not believe their eyes when they found in their hands the sum of . . .—but perhaps it's better not to say how much it was. And immediately they were gripped by a sudden fear, because of a problem that none of them had thought of before: how were they to persuade Lucaroni to accept the money? How should they behave when they handed it to him?

They had underestimated his old ability to solve even the stickiest problems. Raffaele Lucaroni passed serenely from this life at the very moment when loving hands, with much hesitation, were offering him the inadequate token of the gratitude of many, a great many, people. And his last gesture, certainly understanding and perhaps forgiving, was to point to his faithful life companion.

That same year brought a happy surprise. A novel by a new writer appeared in all the bookstores and was a critical success: *In contumacia* (By Default) by Giacoma Limentani. It is an exciting story, written with great skill, with roots that lie in the most private sufferings of a woman—and in a drama that many people experienced, the German occupation of Rome. Many re-experienced that suffering in reading it, and perhaps also wept, but some surely remembered Giacometta when she appeared on the stage, the very image of splendid youth, and sang a popular tune of the time, the "Woodcutter's Song."

On the copy she gave to one of her friends, she wrote: "We've stopped playacting, now we write."